Chubot, the Cursed One

&

Other Stories

Christopher Okemwa

Nsemia

First Edition: December 2011
Published by Nsemia Inc. Publishers (www.nsemia. com)

Edited By: Jennifer Amoah
Cover Concept & Illustration: Robert Kambo Maina
Cover Design: Danielle Pitt
Layout Design: Kemunto Matunda

Note for Librarians:
A cataloguing record for this book is available from Library and Archives Canada.

ISBN: 978-1-926906-15-7

Dedication

To

Those who can forgive

Acknowledgments

I thank Professor Henry Indangasi for taking his time to write a preface to this collection of stories. He also edited them and provided useful pieces of advice.

I also thank Mr. Kimingichi Wabende for his opinion on four of the stories: The Cowardly Girl, The Beautiful Red Bag, Let It Live & Nkatha's Changing Fortunes.

My thanks go to all my other readers that provided insightful feedback on the stories. I am grateful for the work of my editors and publisher that guided the evolution of this work to a state where it is reality.

About the Author

Christopher Okemwa is a poet, actor, dancer, playwright, story-teller, short-story and children's story writer. He graduated from Kamagambo Teachers' Training College and has taught for several years in Kenya. He later graduated from the University of Nairobi with a Bachelor of Education degree, specializing in English and Literature. He also holds an MA degree in literature from the same University. He is currently undertaking doctoral studies at Moi University with research focusing on performance of poetry in Kenya.

He has published two collections of poetry: Toxic Love, and *The Gong*. He has three collections of children's stories: *The Village Queen, The Visitor at the Gate*, and *Let Us Keep Tiger*. Let Us Keep Tiger was nominated for Jomo Kenyatta Prize for Literature in 2011.

Okemwa is a well-known playwright and actor. He has scripted and presented award-winning plays and poems at Kenya Schools Drama Festivals. As a respected drama and literary critic he has published numerous articles in the dailies, journals and newsletters. In 1991, he attended and participated in a theatre and technical workshop in Bristol and Winchester, which was sponsored by the National Operatic & Dramatic Association of England.

Okemwa has also attended and performed his poetry in international poetry festivals, including XX International Poetry Festival in Medellin, Colombia. In 1993 he participated in a poetry workshop in Northern Ireland.

Awards he has won include the 2002 Editor's Choice Award for Outstanding Achievement in Poetry, presented by the International Library of Poetry, and the 2006 Changamoto Arts Fund award for the performance of his poetry in Secondary Schools in Kenya.

Preface

Regarded as the novel's younger cousin, the short story has suffered from critical neglect. It is true that the secondary school English syllabus has a place for this genre. It is also true that the typical literature syllabus in our universities grudgingly acknowledges the existence of the short story. But if truth be told, we pay lip service to the generic integrity of this literary form. We teach the short story the way we teach the novel. We ask students about characterization, stylistic features, and themes the same features they are supposed to look for in the novel but we rarely ask them about the intrinsic nature of the short story. Critics have not paid sufficient attention to the defining features of this genre, and the result is that they do not bother to evaluate the aesthetic achievement and success of any one short story or a collection of them.

Our local publishers have been influenced by the attitude and behaviour of critics and teachers of English. They publish anthologies of short stories for the school market. But they hardly publish a collection from a single author. The view of the planners and policy-makers in the Ministry of Education is that you will use the anthology to learn about the various places represented in the selection. The aesthetics of the short story and the quality of life affirmed in the work are never taken into account. Besides, it is impossible to appreciate the sustained and overall achievement of any one practitioner.

It is against this background that we need to welcome Christopher Okemwa's collection of short stories called *Chubot, the Cursed One and Other Stories*. In these stories, we meet in Okemwa a good storyteller, one who is interested in the supposedly "primitive" art of simply telling a good story. We can say many things about the defining characteristics of human beings; but if we don't mention our universal love of a well-told story, then we miss out on a quality that is intrinsic to human nature. Okemwa is a superlatively gifted storyteller. He is skillful at creating suspense and picking out the interesting detail. He also displays a talent for encapsulating moments of epiphany —moments when an essential truth about human experience is revealed. A short story is about something that happens to someone, which then lays bare an internal truth about the human condition. Stories in the collection do just that.

The lead story, *Chubot, the Cursed One*, is an artistically compelling treatment of Kenya's post-election violence of 2008. We have to admit that it is difficult for Kenyan writers to turn the anger and frustration of this tragic period into a believable work of art. It is difficult to acquire the necessary aesthetic distance to tell the story of the darkest times in our post-independence history. And yet Okemwa has told the harrowing story of a Kikuyu woman's search for her sister, who, though initially believed to be in a hospital in Eldoret, is killed by a Kalenjin. But because of the taboo associated with the shedding of blood in Kalenjin culture, the murderer has cracked up. The irony of the story is that the Kalenjin must look for a relative of the victim to cleanse the murderer-turned-lunatic. In the dramatic rendition of the cleansing ceremony, there is, undoubtedly, a powerful message of reconciliation between the Kikuyu and Kalenjin communities in particular and Kenyan ethnic groups in general.

This Preface is an overview of what the reader will find in this collection of short stories. But although Okemwa's unique voice can be heard all across the collection, each story can and does stand alone as a work of art. Each story has its own unique moments of epiphany; each story reveals something of its own of who we are as human beings. And together, the stories advance the moral imperative of our common humanity.

Henry Indangasi
Professor of Literature
University of Nairobi

The Cowardly Girl

That night Nyamoita did not sleep a wink. She kept turning over and over in her creaking bamboo bed, trying to avoid a petrifying thought that raced up and down her mind like a speeded-up movie reel. She tried to shrug it off, but the more she did so, the more the thought became persistently palpable, sticking itself on her mind like thick glue, gnawing into her head like a malignant tumour.

She flung away her blanket, slipped off the bed and stood on the earthen floor, barefooted, trembling. With nervous fingers, she lit the tin lamp on the small table and the shadow of her nude body threw itself out, stretching on the clay wall beside her, like an ogre. She knew it was only a matter of minutes before that hour came. Her heart palpitated and she shook with terror.

She was ten, the age at which she had to face the knife according to the tradition of her community, the *Abagusii*. She had been aware of this event that now lay before her, and from which she had no power to escape, since she was seven. Big girls and women in the village discussed it extensively and each time she heard the topic she became jittery and frightened.

"Nyamoita, you are yet to face the ogre that will make you a woman," they would say.

"You will be expected to be tough," another would add. "If you scream you will become a curse to our community."

Now the time had come for her to face the ogre that would make her a woman. She had to brave it, face it with courage and preen herself on it later. She brought herself down to her bed and cuddled her little body in remorse. Suddenly all hell broke loose. Noise! Noise! Noise! Noise gathered at a distance. Beats of drumming filled the air. Ululations! Shouts of mockery! The combination grew louder and huge and became a bombshell that quaked the floor beneath her feet, shook her bed and swayed the walls of her hut. Her small frame of body rocked and shattered. Tears flowed down her cheeks, uncontrollably.

The women were now outside her hut. They shouted her out. She quickly opened the door, naked, shaking like a leaf in the wind. Peering quickly into the pool of darkness she could make out hundreds of human beings: old women, young, newly married wives and mature girls. Cuddled and shivering among them were her age mates.

She had hardly stepped outside the door when she was hit by a freezing splash of water. "That is to make you ready for the ogre!" a figure in the dark carrying a pail shouted. "The ogre eats you well only when numb."

Nyamoita and the other girls were led down to the river like goats being taken to a slaughterhouse. They crossed a one-plank bridge in a single file and then followed a narrow path up a gentle hill.

They reached a market road that encircled the village of Bogiakumu, separating it from Bonyando, the neighbouring village. The women sang and danced along, yelling, chanting and shouting obscene words and expressions at the girls.

"This is the same road we followed thirty years ago," one woman said, mockingly, "when we were going to face the ogre."

"I trekked on this same road, this same time, forty years ago," another one prided.

Nyamoita listened to the women's conversation and she cringed. She thought about the ogre--the rusty, crude and cruel knife--and this filled her with fright.

After a long trek they were now in a dark forest, in a chilly mist-filled valley surrounded by small green hills on both sides. Frogs could be heard croaking and dogs barking from a distance. Cocks crowed from the villages on the hillside, heralding the new day. Farmers yelling at their oxen could be heard from farms below the dark rolling fields.

In the glade, the girls were lined up like roasted fish for sale. In a prone position, the ground beneath was freezing and sticky. A short stout woman came along with rise, a poisonous plant and, with it, splashed cold water on their bodies. Their skins itched and pained and made them wriggle in anguish. No girl was supposed to scratch her back to ease the pain. To be seen moving one's hand was itself taboo and one risked being beaten to unconsciousness by the women. One was expected to be firm and unwavering.

Then a song and dance erupted from among the women, more intense this time. The song filled the forest and rent the air above, spreading over the village of Bogiakumu, informing everyone that the ceremony had began and was actually underway and therefore no

man or boy of whatever household, creed or race should graze his cows, work or linger nearby the *egesarero*, the initiation valley, or else, as the women put it in innuendoes, one risked "seeing the invisible," "feeling the intangible" and "hearing the inaudible."

As Nyamoita stretched out on her belly she could hear cries and screams coming from the other end of the line of girls. "Stop screaming and look up!" a voice shouted. "Stupid girl, allow the ogre to eat you!" another voice added. "Let go the ogre! Let go the ogre!" more voices screamed in unison. The exercise had begun, no doubt. Every girl had to be eaten by the ogre and pour blood and appease the ancestral spirits and pay back debts owed, as the belief was, to the ants. It was time for the girls to become nubile, shaped into women, ready to be married and bear children. It was time to shed off the garment of childhood and put on the garment of adulthood.

Cheers for the brave ones, jeers for the cowards, all filled the air, intermingling with the song, producing a concoction of noise that sounded eerie and unearthly upon Nyamoita's ears. It would be a matter of minutes before her turn came. Her numb fingers clutched at the undergrowths beside her head and she shut her eyes tight in fear. Her tiny body quivered and shook. Tears flowed freely and moistened the bare earth below. Her body became stiff, gripped with terror and horror. She held her breath and her heart almost stopped beating. She saw death coming and lost all hope.

She contemplated running away from this anguish. Had she not been taught at school of the adverse effects of this ritual? What of the unnecessary pain she had to endure? She imagined the possibility of bleeding to death or, later, a huge lump growing on her organ like the one she had seen on other circumcised girls when they bathed at the river Mogusii. Running away from this place was one and only option available. She would spring up onto her feet as quickly as thunder, she thought, and in a split second disappear from the place. Run very fast. Run into the thick forest and vanish. The old women, infirm and frail, could be sure not to find their way through the dense woods. She would speed up through the forest, wriggle through the jungle, crawl and creep under the fences, fly over the hedgerows and push down the palisades. She would be safe. She would never regret it.

But then, where was she to run to? What would people say? What would be her mother's reaction? Rumours would do the rounds in the village. Everyone would talk about it. Her age mates would laugh and laugh, laugh and beat their thighs, laugh till tears and mucus flow. Her name would be on everyone's lips. The children in the village and the grandchildren to be born would all be told this story about Nyamoita, the cowardly girl. It would be a story for all generations to come. Her parents would be the scorn of the village. They would be mocked and derided at village social gatherings. They would be referred to as parents of *enkuri* and beer pots and milk gourds would be withdrawn from them in contempt. Meat plates and porridge mugs would quickly be grabbed and hidden under the tables, away from their eyes. They would be viewed as unclean and unfit to share in the village functions. The father would curse the day he married Nyamoita's mother; the mother on the other hand would wish she never bore the pain at Nyamoita's birth.

No, she couldn't afford to let everyone down. Nyamoita was not going to run away. She would stay and endure the anguish. She would brave it for the sake of her parents, her friends and the village as a whole.

The girl, third from her, could be heard writhing and grappling with the women. She could be heard kicking, biting and tearing into their clothes. "Sit up right!" a nervous murmur came. "Hold her hands! Her hands, women!" someone shouted. "Grab her legs! Her legs, women!" another anxious voice burst forth. A fierce struggle ensured. Nyamoita listened to every word, every sound and voice and, for a moment, she thought she was dreaming. She held her breath and stiffened her fingers on the ground, so tightly that she heard them snap. She was now sure to be engulfed, to be swallowed into the underworld. The ground beneath her shook and swayed, crushed and crumbled and she seemed to fall through into the hollowness, screaming and shouting for help. No one came to her aid. No God was around. Neither was her mother. Ghostly drums seemed to beat in her head, clogging her ears and, for a brief moment, she was shut off from the world, from reality.

Suddenly, the girl next to her burst into a loud, sharp scream that rent the air in the dark forest and brought the women's song and dance into a sudden halt. Nyamoita froze with horror. Sweat trickled down her nape, and she could feel it accumulating at the tip of her chin. There was one choice for her. She decided to do one thing. She was determined. She will never regret...

"Stop her! Stop her! She has gone! Run! Women run! It is a shame! Curse! Curse upon her! Curse upon us women! Curse upon the village of Bogiakumu! ..."

These are the words Nyamoita heard behind her as she flew into the dark forest, jumped over the fence and crawled under another, wriggled through the dense woods, flew over the hedgerows and pushed down the palisades, then finally came to the wide road leading to the chief's camp that was situated nearby. She ran along the road, her heart pounding in her like a drum. She reached the gate of the chief's camp. The policemen on night duty were surprised to see a young girl clutching at and pushing the gate.

"This must be another case of a girl escaping from circumcision rite," one policeman quickly thought, as both moved towards the grilled gate.

"Oh, God, too many cases these days!" the other sadly noted.

The two policemen opened the gate for the little girl. Nyamoita was panting and was out of breath as she explained to the two men what had happened. They had heard it before from so many other girls and there was no need of demanding the details from her. She was immediately taken to the other girls who were living in the compound in what Nyamoita heard was the rescuing centre for girls who had escaped from forced circumcision.

The dawn slipped away and the morning came. Nyamoita and the other girls in the rescuing centre were being talked to by some female counsellors when her name was called. She looked up and saw, far away in the field, her father and mother in the company of three policemen and the area chief. She stood up straight, trembling, and walked towards them. When she reached them, she was shocked to see her parents' in handcuffs. They looked remorseful. Both looked down to the ground, without uttering a word. Her mother raised her head and turned towards her:

"Nyamoita, my daughter," she spoke in a low voice. "I am not going to blame you for what happened this morning." She then bent her head and her face turned black with bitterness. "You have brought shame to our family," she said, and broke into tears. The policemen looked on, unstirred, while the father shook his head. "Now you are under the care of the government," she went on and, lowering her head, beads of tears coursed down her cheeks. "Work hard my daughter in whatever you do, and make your dreams come true," she gasped amid tears. "Fill the gap you created this morning." She paused and looked into her face. "With us, your Pa and I, shall serve ten years behind bars." Before she could utter another sentence, the policemen bundled her and the old man into the Land Rover that stood nearby and drove them away towards the gate. Nyamoita, shocked and tongue-tied, walked back to join the other girls in the counselling room.

Kitendawili

Adhiambo lived in the Kibera slum, on the sixteenth alley, in a small two bed-roomed house. She had two daughters and a son. To earn a living she sold ground nuts by the roadside and begged for alms from passers-by. Every evening after her work at the road side she would send her two daughters, Atieno and Aoko, to the street to beg for alms. One evening she closed her ground nut business early and came home to prepare her daughters to go out as usual.

Atieno and Aoko had just come from school when they heard, *"Kitendawili?"* It was their mother.

"Tega!" they all replied and ran towards the door, bubbling with joy. They were used to communicating in innuendoes, insinuations and allusions; their conversations were heavily coded, and only they could understand one another.

"You are going out today," she said. "Yesterday you did very well. With your success I am able to buy each one of you a pair of shoes. Last week, too, you did well. I am sure today you will use your wit to get something extraordinarily big." Then, flagging them off, she said: "Go pick a pocket or two, or three, or four. Come home safely, dear." She kissed each one of them on the back of their hands as she normally did.

The two flew into their bedroom and came out clad in their night dresses and hooded sweaters. *"Kitendawili?"* they bid their mother and brother bye.

"Tega!" the old lady and the younger brother responded.

They hurried down to the Mfangano Street which was usually crowded by people who were doing their late and last-minute shopping for the day. These were mostly working class people who had to carry vegetables home, or some missing commodity for their kitchen. Mfangano Street was also known for its congested shops and kiosks, open market for second hand clothing and as a meeting place for adolescent boys and girls. As a result of the latter it was also called Love Street.

Here, Atieno and Aoko mingled among the people, looking up to see those in smart suits and those carrying heavy luggage. They checked about for women who carried expensive handbags in their hands. Anyone with a Nokia phone was an automatic target. They were intelligent little girls whose sharp eyes roved with dexterity and experience; they were capable of catching a glimpse of the "right cow to be milked" that evening. They were quick to listen to conversations of groups of people who either were buying or selling, and would make a quick decision as to whether they were worth something.

"Kitendawili!" Atieno whispered.

"Tega!" Aoko replied in an undertone, and quickly followed her. Atieno moved close to a tall dark bushy-bearded man who was busy scratching a phone card with his coin while holding his phone with the same hand with which he was scratching. He was standing next to a long rickety wooden table on the narrow path that was crammed with passers-by. Atieno squeezed herself

beside him and stood in front and below his armpit and pretended to be looking at something to buy. There were second-hand cups, mugs, tooth-brushes, pens, exercise books and shoes. As she rubbed against the man's belly, Aoko skillfully inserted her two fingers into his coat pocket and successfully removed a purse. She then slipped away quickly.

"Kitendawili!" she said as she weaved her way among the people, disappearing down the narrow muddy path. Atieno on hearing the remark, followed her with great speed. They went to the vast Mboya Park. Bubbling with anxiety and joy for the success, they opened the purse. Alas! It contained only papers: an Identity Card and a Personal Identification Number Certificate. There was no money in it. Not a cent. Disappointed, they cursed!

Then they hurled the purse into the middle of the field and rushed back to Mfangano Street.

Once on the street, they saw a woman who was buying vegetables. Her handbag was dangling from her right shoulder. This time Aoko went to the front. She quickly removed her razor blade from her hooded jacket and moved closer to her. She at once ran the blade across below the zip, and then stood in front of her to obstruct her from concentrating on the handbag; Atieno got the chance and quickly inserted her two fingers into the torn bag and pulled out a mobile phone and a handkerchief.

She slithered away quickly. *"Kitendawili!"* she said as she squeezed through the mass of people. Upon hearing the hint, Atieno left the place in haste and followed her sister. When they reached the Mboya Park, which by now was covered in darkness, Aoko took out the mobile phone. Once in her hand, it rang and sent them into panic. "The owner is ringing, Aoko! *Iweke off upesi!"* Aoko immediately put it off and quickly slit it open and removed the SIM card. "This is about seven thousand shillings," Aoko whispered, heaving a sigh of satisfaction. "Mom will be happy with us."

"She will be grateful," Atieno added, taking in a deep breath and letting it out in a whoosh of excitement.

They once again set off to Mfangano Street. It was now totally dark and few people were lounging about. Even those selling vegetables and clothes had packed their wares and were counting their money ready to leave for their homes. Atieno and Aoko now lacked the crowd to shield them from being seen as they carried out their clandestine activities. They strolled, seemingly relaxed and, purposelessly, darting their eyes here and there, and talking to those sellers who had packed and were waiting for the parking boys to collect their wares for storage. At times they would take time to flirt with the street boys who were also out to get a kill. At the far corner of the market was lying something like a carton left on its own. Aoko noticed it from where they were walking and alerted Atieno. "Atieno, *kitendawili!*" she whispered.

"Tega!" Atieno replied moving close to Aoko to find out what opportunity was at sight. Aoko then pointed her hand over yonder. "You see it?"

"Yes," Atieno whispered.

They both hurried toward the spot, each one walking in her own direction to avoid being noticed. They converged where the object was. Sure enough it was a carton wrapped in a black polythene paper with a thick sisal rope tautly running round it. Aoko stood beside it intending to have her legs conceal it from being seen by people in the market. Atieno bent down to touch and feel what was inside. *"Kitendawili?"* Aoko asked.

"I can't tell what it is," replied Atieno, as she pressed the corners of the carton. "Let us just carry it all the same," Atieno concluded. Atieno curved her index finger into a hook and placed it under the sisal rope and lifted the carton up, then started walking with it toward the far end-corner of the market. Aoko followed, looking in all directions for anyone who might notice or who might be approaching. No one was looking in their direction and no one approached. The darkness was now thicker than it was at the beginning and they could not be seen from a distance. They placed the carton under the fence and squeezed their small bodies through a narrow opening in the fence. They came out through the other side and were now on the main road. They walked quickly beside the road on the tall grass.

Suddenly they saw a man running towards them. Aoko suddenly threw the carton down and was ready to run, while Atieno had started crossing the road, ready to flee. But the man crushed past them and did not even notice the abandoned carton. They quickly picked it up and walked faster up the road. They branched to the right, walking along the sewage water that moved in a snail's pace down to the road. They reached the narrow alley that snaked between two rows of buildings. Their house stood on the right of the alley in the middle of others. They climbed the rough porch and swung the untidy curtain that hung on the doorway and went into the house. They dropped the carton on the floor and both heaved a sigh of relief, and wiped their sweating faces.

"Kitendawili, mama!" Atieno and Aoko spoke spontaneously together, their faces bright with joy.

"Tega, my daughters!" mother spoke and came forward to meet them, her chest heaving in anticipation.

They opened the carton with abated breath. The sisal rope was so tight and its knots were hard to undo. Their young brother brought a knife and cut the sisal twine tying the carton. Inside the carton was another layer of polythene that was also tied with a sisal rope. They cut this as well. "What can this be!" their mother wondered loudly, as her daughters looked on with anxiety. Adhiambo pressed the polythene paper to feel the thing inside. It felt soft and amorphous. She took in a deep breath and let it out in a whoosh of bewilderment. Her fingers were nervous and her head felt heavy upon her neck. "What can this be!" she wondered again, her daughters getting uneasy with her anxiety. "Mummy, are you worried what might be inside here?" the young boy asked. No one responded. They peeled one more layer of polythene and then tore the last one. Uh-oh--There! A brown thing! Eyes! Nose! Mouth! Legs! What? A baby girl? Is she dead? Is she alive? What the hell!

"Atieno, Aoko, what hell is this?" their mother screamed, perplexed.

"Mummy eh!" Atieno exclaimed, moving back.

"Oh, Mummy!" Aoko said, her mouth gaping, clutching her cheeks in her palms.

"Remove the wrapping to unveil the head!" the lady cried, confused. Atieno's trembling fingers pulled the polythene away. The head and the black hair were visible. All four stood back and watched in disbelief. They were transfixed on the floor, tongue-tied, shaking like grass in the wind. Adhiambo looked on and for a moment she thought she was dreaming. What has hell brought to our house today? This is bad luck! What can we do now? Oh my God!

The first thing that came to her mind was to throw the baby outside in the alley. But, oh no! It was still early and someone was bound to see her carrying the thing. She decided to throw it in the dust bin outside their house, so that the litter collector would take it away in the morning. She summoned everyone to go to sleep so that she could manage the tragedy alone. The girls and the boy left without a word, tongue-tied, shocked and dazed.

Alone, she wrapped back the polythene papers and tied the carton with fresh sisal ropes that she pulled from her old baskets. She then brought a big sack from under her bed and stashed the carton into it. She then carried the load towards the door. As she stood at the threshold, she could see that people were still walking along the long winding alley. Also in houses next to the alley, lamps were still burning. If she threw the carton in the dust bin outside, she would be noticed by a neighbour through the window or by a passer-by walking along the alley. She hesitated in the threshold and finally decided to recede into the house.

She sat panting, lost in deep thought. She was confused, apprehensive and bewildered. At some moment she dozed on the chair where she was sitting. At about midnight, Adhiambo peeped through the door to study the situation outside. It was quiet. The lights from the wooden windows had long been extinguished. The music from the shops and adjacent houses had long died. It was safe, she thought. She would now walk out comfortably and, without an iota of self-consciousness or suspicion, push the carton into the dust bin and come back and get to bed.

As she placed the carton in the bin, she suddenly remembered that the following day was a Sunday and the litter collector could not come for the waste until Monday morning. Surely the dead baby could not stay in the bin the whole day. It needed urgent disposal. The dust bin could not help. She lifted the carton from the bin, heaving, and held it firmly in her hands. She tottered into the house. She sat on a chair and took in a deep breath and let it out quietly. She was filled with so many thoughts that crisscrossed in and out of her mind.

Oh, yes--the toilet! She could throw it in there and it could be safe. The toilet was shared with the neighbours, but no one was going to look into the hole every time she or he used it after all. She took a torch and carried it in one hand while the other hand held the carton tightly under her arms. She tiptoed out, and jumped over the sewage stream that flowed gently down the alley; she was completely oblivious of the stench. She reached the toilet. She pulled the door towards her slowly, and entered into the tiny space. She flashed her torch into the hole and noticed a conglomeration of worms, making something like froth of beer. She then squeezed the carton through the hole, stepped on it with her foot and it finally went through--Pu! The sound was so loud that she thought someone had heard it. She put off her torch and stood silently for a while, listening to the crackling silence of the night and the pant of her own urgent breathing. She flashed her torch into the hole again. Much to her chagrin, she saw that the carton had not sunk into the faeces. She flashed her torch into the hole again, and stayed looking in there for a long time, not knowing what to do. The carton had not sunk, but was floating on the worms. The human waste appeared to refuse to 'swallow' the thing. Maybe, during the night, she thought, the worms would crawl over it and by the following day it would be concealed. She had her fingers crossed and went back to the house.

In her bed, she was too tense and uneasy to sleep. The night hummed with moths and insects as she lay between the sheets, listening to the croaking of frogs from the sewerage system nearby and the creak of wooden structures outside the house. In a daze, she dreamed of vampires and ghosts, of people shouting and admonishing her. At one time in her nightmares, she thought she heard the baby scream from inside the toilet, and saw people coming towards her to beat her up for throwing away someone's baby. And at times she heard the baby sing from where she lay dead, and at other times she heard it laughing so hysterically, mystery and wonder in her voice.

At two o'clock in the morning, Adhiambo startled up from her sleep. She had been dreaming that policemen had come to search for the dead baby and she was found with it. She was sweating all over her body. She jumped out of bed and tiptoed towards the door which she opened; it was dark outside. Leaving the door ajar, she tiptoed back and picked up the torch from where she had kept it early in the night, on the small table. She came to the door and peeped outside. Gathering courage, she stealthily walked towards the toilet. Once there she opened the door and silently stood on the toilet floor. She then flashed her torch into the hole. Much to her chagrin and shock, the carton had not sunk an inch. She trembled. She became nervous and her mind went blank. The carton lay there like a big monster, a devil of a thing, a ghost, a witch, a …..She felt like screaming. She thought of shouting "A baby! A baby in the toilet! Come all and see!" But people were not going to believe her. She went out and took a long stick and tried to push the thing down, below the worms. It only stirred, but remained adamant, defying all her effort even with the use of the stick.

It was dawn; the cocks could be heard crowing from a distance. In an hour's time people would start walking along the narrow alley past the toilet. She had to decide what to do, and do it immediately. She decided to retrieve the carton and bring it to the house, keep it there until she found the right thing to do. She walked back to the house, lowered her body and placed her head on the floor. She then shone her torch under her bed. There was a sisal rope. She crawled under the bed and pulled it out. She then picked up a piece of wire that was lying in the corner of their house. She bent it into a hook. She then tied the sisal rope to the wire hook. She walked out of the house and went to the toilet. The night was still silent and dark. The stars looked grimacing on the sky. The wind that blew by sounded like a dirge. Once in the toilet, she lowered the sisal rope and reached the carton. Good God! The hook caught one strand of the sack; she then pulled the sisal rope and-- thank God in all things! -- the whole thing came straight up with a minor struggle and nudge through the pit hole. She heaved a sigh of relief as she carefully placed the carton on the floor of the toilet. With her body trembling, she examined this monster which had defied all her architecture and physics. Worms were crawling all over it. She cleaned the worms and the faeces with the newspapers that were hung from the roof of the toilet that were used by people who could not afford the toilet tissue. She then carried the carton that was jeweled with pearls of crawling worms into the house.

She laid the carton under her bed. It emitted a pungent stench which, she imagined, could be felt a hundred miles away. She feared that the neighbours would get the whiff of the foul smell through the windows of their houses. She closed the window so that the smell could not go out. But the smell was suffocating, so stinking that it woke up the children. "Mummy," Aoko called, as she came through the doorway that led to their room. "It stinks." Atieno and the little boy followed Aoko, and all stood, gazing at their mother. They had not been asleep all this time, but had been engulfed in terror even as they listened to their mother's goings in and out. Adhiambo asked Atieno to open the only window that faced the alley.

It was now six in the morning. Mama Njeri, a neighbour, came knocking at their door. "Adhiambo! Adhiambo!" she called. Adhiambo opened the door with trembling fingers; her breath came thickly, quickly. "Adhiambo," she started, "did you hear the commotion last night?" Adhiambo's lips became dry.

"Wha, wha, what co-commotion?" her lips felt stiff and frozen, she could not find the words. She shook with fear, the colour receding from her face, leaving it as white as the marble wall.

"Something or someone was moving to and from the toilet."

"Oh---!" she exclaimed and stopped. Her mouth seemed to be coated with sand.

"Something was going on; I could not tell what it was."

"Well, I didn't hear anything," she spoke and her throat closed with panic. Suppose they already know? Suppose one of them had opened the window last night and spotted my figure? Maybe they know, they do, surely they do...

As the two women spoke, the waft of the foul smell came steadily through the door, and even an insensitive nose could not miss out on this stench. Adhiambo's face told the whole story: Pallid, flushed, twitching, red eyes, unkempt hair...

"Let me ask Mama Okello if she heard the noise," Mama Njeri excused herself and walked away. Adhiambo stood there, transfixed, shaking like a bedraggled mongrel. She fidgeted, looked around for any betraying clues: sewage marks on the wall, on the door and on the floor; the intense stench coming from inside; the pieces of worms stamped into smithereens on the veranda... would they see all these pieces of evidence?

Mama Okello could be seen peeping from the door. Mama Njeri leaned forward as she talked to her. They were talking in lower voices. Whispers and gestures were all directed towards Adhiambo. Adhiambo followed their suspicious conversation from the corner of her eye. Her temples pounded and the palms of her hands sweated. Mama Njeri came back to Adhiambo. "Mama Okello says she also heard the noise."

"Sure!" Adhiambo said and her heart increased in tempo and every beat drummed in pain. She trembled and for a brief moment she saw darkness descending upon her. Her heart sunk.

"She says that the noise was heard by everyone."

"I never heard anything myself."

"It is only you who never heard anything," she said. "The rest of us followed it clearly throughout the night." Mama Njeri hesitated a bit before leaving, her head downcast as though she had got a clue to her many questions. Adhiambo entered her house, checked around with trembling lips, then brought her body down to the floor to check the monster that lay under the bed: terrifying, frightening. Her heart sunk.

Atieno and Aoko had put on their school uniforms and were ready to go to school. She looked up at them and was shocked to realize that she was going to be left all alone with that demon. "You are going to school?" she asked, her voice coming from a hundred miles outside her body.

"Yes, Mummy, what else can we do?" Atieno responded remorsefully. The two girls and their younger brother left the house. They had not gone far when Adhiambo was hit by an idea: She could have given them the carton to throw away on their way to school. She grabbed the carton, and in a split second, she was staggering out with it, calling "Atieno! Aoko! Wait! Wait! Wait!"

The neighbours quickly came to their doors, windows, staring, as she ran along the filthy alley, carefully clutching the stinking, flayed and dirty carton. "Stop! take this along with you! Stop, Aoko! Stop Atieno!"

"Mummy, no!" cried Atieno, trembling, confused.

"Mummy, just keep it in the house!" said Aoko, almost in tears.

"Take! Take! Take! Take it stupid girls!"

"No Mummy!" Atieno pleaded, the words coming out like a scream.

"Take it now! Throw it somewhere," she mumbled, with a tone of urgency, looking around, confused, mad.

The neighbours had now moved from their doors and had assembled outside their houses, watching with suspicion, wander and dismay. A small murmur started among them as they watched Adhiambo shoving the carton on Atieno. "Mummy, I can't! I can't!" She pleaded, gesturing with bewilderment and pain.

"You will take it and throw it somewhere. Okay?"

"No Mummy," Atieno cried, overwhelmed. She held the carton, her mouth gaping, lost, confused.

The stench of the carton could be caught from many miles away. The neigbours had been joined by passers-by, and they had formed a big crowd on the alley. "What is that carton carrying by the way?" one of them was heard asking.

"We need to know," another added.

"We must know what that carton contains," another one remarked. The whole crowd charged, moving quickly towards Adhiambo and her two daughters. "Adhiambo, stop, don't force them to take it away," one man shouted. Atieno stood transfixed on the spot, heaving, holding the carton in her hands. She looked around suspiciously. Confused thoughts span and whirled in Adhiambo's head, and suddenly she began pulling hair from her head. Aoko was sobbing and pulling at the hem of her skirt. Suddenly Atieno threw the carton down and ran away, followed by Aoko. Adhiambo stood there, fiercely pulling hair from her head, bewildered and mad.

"What is inside here, Adhiambo?" one man commanded.

"The- " she said, but the words stuck in her throat.

"Open it now!" another commanded.

Women, with children on their backs, moved closer. The sellers at the market also ran in to see. The shopkeepers banged doors of their shops and quickly locked them and ran in to find out. The passengers in buses alighted and craved to catch the story. The *bodaboda* men slowed down their motorcycles and stopped to hear what was happening. There was a huge crowd. As this multitude surged forward towards

Adhiambo, a deafening squeal was heard, followed by a loud screech, both of which snuffed out the noise of the crowd. A Landrover had pulled up behind them. Four policemen on patrol came out with their guns totting.

"What is going on here?" one of them asked, as people gave way for them to come forward.

"This mama has a carton that is—" one woman started and her words were swallowed by the jostling and shoving crowd.

"Mama, hii mzigo ni ya nini?" a second policeman inquired.

One man in the crowd suddenly burst forward, volunteering to unravel the mystery in the carton. He took the carton and fiercely tore the first layer of polythene paper that wrapped it. People looked on with abated breath. The women in the crowd clutched their cheeks in their palms. Men gaped, tongue-tied. Young men cried with horror. Children looked on, perplexed, confused. The young man then untied a sisal rope that ran round the second layer. He then tore the second layer of polythene with his nails. People filled their lungs with air. He finally rolled out the last layer. Oh! What? A head! Two eyes! Legs! A baby girl! What the hell is this! The crowd went crazy, crying for the blood of the poor widow. *"Taya!"* some men shouted. *"Petroli!"* loud voices filled the air. *"Kiberiti!"* voices shouted in unison.

The policemen shot in the air and the crowd took cover. *"Mama, twende uelezee mbele,"* one policeman said with a tone of urgency. They bundled her into the Landrover and drove away with her and the carton, with the dead baby's head protruding.

Chubot, the Cursed One

Njeri received a call from an anonymous person who told her that her sister in Eldoret, was in Hospital. "She is in critical condition!" the nervous voice came. "She is suffering from wounds sustained from burns when her house was razed. Please come with her daughter."

"Who?-what, a-a-a—" before Njeri could ask for clarification, the caller hung up. Efforts to call the number back were fruitless. "The subscriber cannot be reached!" the voice came. Njeri stood there, motionless. She looked at her mobile phone, took in a deep breath and let it out nervously. Her sister, Nyambura? Her house razed? She feared the worst. Eldoret was the epicentre of unrest and mayhem after the election, and Njeri wondered whether her sister was really alive as the caller claimed. She must be dead, she said to herself, and beads of tears danced in her eyeballs. She stopped stirring the porridge and left the kitchen. She sat on the sofa and cupped her cheeks in her palms.

Nyambura, having divorced her husband ten years earlier, left for Eldoret where she bought a piece of land and built rental houses. She also owned several businesses in Eldoret and the suburbs. Some time while living in Eldoret, she developed an interest in politics and had just contested a civic seat from Asegisegi ward on a Party of National Unity ticket, the result of which had not come because the election was disputed and this had contributed to the violence in various parts of the country.

She had spent almost two hours in a trance, utterly lost in history, social issues and economic woes the country and, in particular, her family members had been experiencing. Her father had died and left them with their mother. That was way back in 1984. Their mother had brought them up on porridge and *githeri*, single-handedly. When they completed secondary school Nyambura got married, but later divorced. Her other sister, Mumbi had a successful marriage and had accepted to take in Nyambura's only daughter, Nelly. The latter had stayed with her since her mother left for Eldoret ten years ago.

Njeri picked up her mobile phone and decided to call her sister, Mumbi. "Have you heard the news? Nyambura is in critical condition in Eldoret Hospital, please let Nelly come very early in the morning," she said. She didn't want to elaborate, or entertain questions. If she gave a chance to Mumbi to express shock, she would make her grow nervous. She hung up.

That night she didn't sleep at all. She was up by the time the cock crowed at three in the morning. But she just lay there waiting for dawn. At five she sprung up, prepared breakfast and set the table. By six Nelly had not come. She ate her breakfast slowly, waiting to hear the knock at the front door. No knock had come by seven o'clock. She watched the news on TV and learnt that so many people, especially the Kikuyus and the Kisiis, had been killed in Eldoret. She crossed her fingers that Nyambura was alive and recovering. One news item said that policemen had shot three young men in Eldoret, but didn't mention their tribe. The situation was volatile. Shall we make it to Eldoret, Njeri wondered.

It was ten and Nelly had not arrived. Njeri thought something had gone wrong. Did Mumbi really give her proper directions? She wondered. Nelly had been to her house several times in the past. Although several buildings had risen in the neighbourhood in the recent past that did not make any difference to anyone quite as observant as Nelly. Maybe she needed to call Mumbi, but she feared the shock she would express and the numerous questions she would ask.

Njeri had started putting on her clothes when a knock finally came. She rushed to open the door. Yes, it was Nelly. "Oh Nelly!" she exclaimed. Nelly removed her shoes at the threshold and hugged her Aunt Njeri held her tightly, closed her eyes and felt the warmth that comes with a daughter as lovely as Nelly.

"Aunt I have missed you. So many years!" she cried.

"Yes, it has been three years," Njeri agreed. She then loosened her grip on Nelly's plumb figure and moved back to look at her in the eyes. "You have grown into a woman," Njeri said, her face lit with joy. Nelly smiled. She held her hand and led her into the house where Nelly slumped into a sofa. "Now, Nelly, I hope Mumbi has explained to you. Someone rang me and said that your mother is in critical condition in Eldoret."

"Yes, she did," Nelly nodded her head.

"Nelly, I fear the worst," Njeri said, and her forehead grew black with two thin wrinkles.

"I, too, have misgivings, Aunt," Nelly said and tears moistened her eyes. She loved her mother very much and had not seen her for many years now. The last time they met was when she came home five years ago to tell them that she would be contesting a civic seat in the following election. Nelly was seven years old then.

After staring at each other for a long time, Njeri sprung up. She served Nelly a cup of porridge which the latter sipped little by little while biting sweet potatoes. The anxiety in her had killed her appetite. Her mind was already visualizing their journey to Eldoret.

Both had finished their preparation by eleven o'clock. At eleven thirty they entered Njeri's car and set off. The watchman closed the gate behind them. The atmosphere from Nairobi to Nakuru was serene, smooth and without the hustles and bustles that characterized the road during other days. There were a few vehicles and almost no pedestrians. Policemen stood at strategic points beside the road, alert, with guns on the ready. When they were about to reach Nakuru they were stopped by five policemen at a roadblock. They were frisked; their car's boot was opened and checked for drugs and weapons. They were finally permitted to go. Nelly was not used to seeing the policemen, and she grew nervous in their presence.

The road from Nakuru to Kericho was not smooth at all.

They crossed five roadblocks. At Kipkelion they bumped into a group of men who were carrying bows and arrows, waving branches of trees, singing "PNU! PNU! PNU!" These were supporters of Party of National Unity and were celebrating the election results which PNU had won. They were drunk, rough and crazy. When they saw Njeri's car they shouted and performed obscene gestures before them. Some peered through the closed windows, and some banged on the body of the car, while one of them hit the car with a stone, breaking the window beside Njeri. Njeri panicked. Nelly saw the panic on her face and she screamed, clinging onto her. "Don't be afraid, Nelly," she emboldened her. Nervous, Njeri steered the car carefully, slithering it amidst the irate crowd and finally squeezed past them. She then sped off once out of the crowd.

Njeri breathed a sigh of relief. They were out of danger. They arrived at Kericho at two. In Kericho there was a lot of commotion. Policemen and the supporters of Orange Democratic Movement were running battles across the town. Tear-gas canisters were flying in the air, gun shots could be heard sporadically, and the "ODM! ODM! ODM!" slogan was echoed across the town and its suburbs.

Njeri pulled up at a petrol station and looked at Nelly. "My daughter, where are we really going?" The voice was shrill, moaning. Nelly was surprised by this question. She didn't understand what Njeri meant.

"Why? We are going to see Mum?" she said, naivety in her voice. Before they could converse more, a drunken tall man appeared from nowhere and stood at the window next to Njeri, peering inside. He was carrying a spear.

"Open the door!" he demanded. Before Njeri could think of what to do five more men had joined him. Ten more appeared. In a few minutes there was a big crowd of people surrounding the car and shouting "ODM! ODM! ODM! Njeri was filled with terror. They were in danger, she thought. Open or we overturn this car!" one of them threatened. Njeri gained courage and opened the door, slipped out of the car and tried to remain composed. Two of the men grabbed her hand and half-dragged her from the others. Nelly started screaming.

"Keep quiet, or else we will beat you," one man roared at Nelly and wielded a sword at her by the window. She kept quiet.

Njeri came back to the car and picked up her handbag, her chest heaving. Out of it she slipped five thousand shillings which she gave to one of the men who must have been their leader.

"*Mama safiri salama*," they said, almost in unison. "*Lakini huko mbele si sawa,*" one of them explained, as others nodded in agreement. All the same Njeri drove away, breathing a sigh of relief.

It was three o'clock when they left Kericho. Nelly was now hungry. Njeri told her to take out some chapatis that were in her handbag and pour some porridge from a thermos into a cup, both of which she had prepared in the morning before Nelly had arrived. In a few minutes, Nelly was munching and sipping away happily, oblivious of the many dangers around them.

Suddenly the weather outside changed. The wind howled through the broken glass with such savage violence that it seemed to be alive. Nelly inserted a carton into it to prevent the cold and water from coming in. She also closed all other windows. Outside they could see whirlwind lifting soil and sticks and depositing them somewhere far from the road. Far away the low trees were black against the fading sky; the orange streaks of sunset were smudged with grey, as if by dirty thumbs.

It was four and the rain had intensified. The road was slippery and Njeri found it hard to be steady. The tyres slid and swayed from side to side. Njeri feared she might cause an accident. She drove slowly and nervously. The rain increased and the wind blew hard on the windscreen. Njeri found it more and more difficult to keep her steering steady. When they arrived at a small market called Kaitui, Njeri drove into a supermarket and pulled into the parking lot. "Let us get out, Nelly," she said, and both leaped out, ran through the rain and entered a pub nearby. They sat and waited for the rain to subside. Inside there were a few men and women who were sipping from glasses. It could have been Guinness, Tusker or Malt lager.

It was seven and the rain continued unabated. As Njeri and Nelly sat forlornly a tall gangling man, dressed in a red *shuka*, carrying a club, came and stood before them. He asked, "Are you strangers here?" Njeri smiled and answered "Yes, why?"

"It is good to know," the man went on. "Are you supporting PNU or ODM?" the man asked, chewed tobacco and inserted some powder into his nostril and sneezed.

"We don't support any of them," she said. "Politicians are just sly foxes; they are not of any benefit to any of us. Whoever goes to parliament, or whoever becomes the president, should be none of our business. They are all the same—selfish!"

The man peered into Njeri's eyes as if he had seen a warthog perch there. He brought himself down on the chair next to her and nodded his head and wore an expression of a face that was in deep meditation. "I love what you are saying, mama. You are very intelligent. *"Wee ni malimu?"* Njeri just smiled. Few people were watching from nearby tables and following bits of their conversation. They were mostly men, with torn ears, clad in *shukas* and carrying clubs in their hands.

"A teacher, no! Just self-employed."

"So, now where are you going?"

"Eldoret?"

"Eldoret? *Utatoboa mama?"* the man expressed surprise.

"Yes, why?" Njeri composed herself, and held Nelly's hand and smoothed it.

"You are kogoyot, are you?"

"Yes, why?"

"Mama wa kogoyot, hawa apana ogopa."

However, the man told her it was dangerous to drive through two town centres ahead of her—Awasi and Kapsabet--and if Njeri really wanted to arrive in Eldoret safely then she had to branch off the main road and drive along a private and less known road. He explained that she had to take Kaitui-Kapsabet road, which deviated from the main road. Although not tarmacked, the road had been spread with murram recently. Njeri thought about it and agreed. When the rain stopped, the man entered their vehicle and showed them the way to Kapsabet. "My home is along that road," he said.

"And what brought you to Kaitui?" Njeri asked, wondering.

"Hapa tunakucha siasa tu," he said.

Nelly was comfortable at the back seat, although she had to lean forward from time to time to catch up with their conversation. They drove for almost half an hour through stony roads. Some parts were muddy and did not have enough stones, so the car swerved from one side to the other, sending Nelly screaming and holding onto Njeri's seat. '*Toto, hapana lia,*" the man would say, baring banana-stained yellow teeth at the girl. At one point they met crowds of people carrying clubs, spears and sticks. "These people will kill you if they know you are a Kogoek," the man said and showed fear on his face. "*Kogoek hapana takikana hapa.*" Njeri's back shuddered, as she negotiated the small space between them, and speeded up after leaving them behind.

The night was thick and dark, the sky starless, and thunder still roared across the hills; lights flushed a little at the windows and Nelly closed her eyes. Njeri drove along. Nelly had started dosing on her seat, oblivious of the place where they were. It was eight o'clock when they arrived at Kapsabet town. The man told Njeri to stop the car. "*Hapa ndio kwangu, unaona?*" he said. He alighted and explained to Njeri the direction she should take.

Njeri started the car and it slid off the road and veered to the side where there was a trench. The tyres skidded, but the more it did the deeper it sunk in its rut. The man, upon seeing smoke going up from the tyres, ran to the back to push the car out. He called upon other men who were passing by in the vain hope that the car would come out of the mud. But the tyres slid and the car leant against the steep road side. "It is going to be difficult to get it out of here," the men observed. Njeri came out of the car and stood beside it to examine the extent to which it had sunk. It was dark in the middle of nowhere. Nelly woke up from her slumber and opened the door and came out. She accidentally stepped on a wet surface, slid and almost fell down in the mud, thanks for the old man's long clammy hands.

The men and Njeri stood there not knowing what to do. It was now nine o'clock. "It would not be possible to get this car out of this sludge," the men were honest with her. Her mind was blank. The old man suggested they spend a night in his home and wake up early in the morning to continue with their journey. "How shall we get it out tomorrow?" Njeri asked the old man.

"I will send for strong boys tonight, and tomorrow they will be here," the old man assured her.

Njeri took all her personal documents from the car and closed all the windows and locked the doors. They followed the old man along a muddy footpath that led into a maize plantation. They were accompanied by two other men who spoke very little and looked timid.

"I have enough bedding for you two," the man assured them. "My third wife will cook enough food for you."

"Njeri smiled in the dark, clutching her bag and paper bag close to herself. Nelly held her hand, walking beside her, wading through the wet grass. They crossed a small valley that had no water flowing through it. They then walked across a vast field with scattered trees. Finally they were able to see three houses afar. "There is my home!" the old man said, pointing in the darkness. The other quiet men came to an abrupt stop. "*saisere, si ketuyen karon*," the man bid them bye. They walked away towards the opposite direction, and disappeared into the darkness.

When they reached the man's home, there was his wife who looked very young. A boy and two daughters were in the kitchen preparing supper. They all showed surprise when they saw Njeri and Nelly stringing along with the old man. "These are our visitors; prepare something for them to eat and a bed for them to sleep," the old man announced. Before the old man completed speaking, a squeaking noise of a cock was heard from the kitchen; the young boy was already grabbing one to slaughter.

In a couple of hours a big 'mountain' of *ugali* was transported to the table in a big bowl. An aluminium holder containing the entire chicken landed on the table. Milk in a huge gourd was placed on the floor next to the table so as to spare the space on the table for other dishes. The milk, as Njeri realized, was not pure milk. "We call this Mursik," the old man explained the odd potpourri of milk, charcoal and blood. "The charcoal in the milk is from a herbal tree," the old man explained.

"It is tasty," Njeri said and smiled.

Nelly didn't talk, but munched her supper silently. The old man's young wife and the children ate their supper in the kitchen, away from the visitors. From time to time the young woman would make a journey to the table to see if her services were needed. "Salt?" she would ask, "water?" If nobody replied, she would go back to the kitchen and continue with her supper. At the end of the meal, a big jug containing porridge was brought to the table. The porridge was served in huge calabashes.

"Where is a TV here?" Nelly asked, but was pinched by her Aunt to keep quiet. Lows and bleats were heard coming from outside: Someone was milking the cows, and tethering the goats and sheep. There was one dog which kept barking since they came in. They also owned one grey cat, which licked *ugali* laced with chicken soup.

A bed had been moved from the old man's bedroom through the back door and placed in Chelagat's house. Chelagat was the only daughter in the home. When they were led to this house, Njeri and Nelly sneezed. The floor seemed to have been swept a few minutes earlier before they came in. The roof was thatched and seemed to leak; there were spots on the earthen floor that had been eroded by water falling from the leaking roof above. The bedroom was partitioned by a thin mat. It didn't have a hearth and therefore was cold.

Njeri placed her bag and purse on the small table Chelagat used for her studies. Nelly asked for the toilet. Chelagat opened the door and went to her parents' house and came with a torch. She escorted her out. The latrine was a little distance from the house.

The compound had many other houses on the right and left of the homestead. They belonged to the man's first and second wives and their children. Nelly had not seen fireflies and this was a spectacle. When they went back to the house she told Njeri about them. "Do they burn, Aunt?" she asked. Njeri smiled, and Chelagat burst into laughter. "Do they bite like mosquitoes?" she enquired further, sending Chelagat into more bouts of laughter.

"Nelly," Njeri said, pulling her close to her, "these are fireflies, they don't burn, nor do they bite."

"We can catch some tomorrow and take them with us. Maybe we can tame them till they grow into big animals," Nelly said, and Njeri laughed loudly this time.

"You won't see them in the morning," Chelagat explained. "They disappear during the day and appear during the night."

"They are nocturnal," Njeri added. "They are seen only at night and not during the day."

They slept in a bed that was made of sisal ropes, which bowed downwards, and brought the two together in the middle. We are not here for comfort, Njeri thought, restraining herself from commenting about the bed. Chelagat slept on a hide on the floor and covered herself with a threadbare piece of blanket.

There were no toilets in the house and Nelly wondered where she was going to relieve herself at night. "Auntie, where shall we go for a short call at night?"

"But, are you not from the toilet, right now?" Nelly didn't reply. "That is all for tonight. You have to endure until tomorrow. After all you have not drunk tea, have you?"

The night was silent unlike in the city where traffic roared throughout the night. The silence was only broken by owls which hooted from bushes below the hills. The barking of dogs also came in faintly. In the morning, birds' chirps from all direction made sweet music that woke up Njeri and Nelly. It was a strange type of morning, unlike the one in the city that was filled up with honking horns, and zooming of *matatus* and motorcycles.

They didn't bother to ask for water to bathe or to wash their faces. They thanked the old man, his wife and children for hosting them. Njeri then bid them bye and were escorted by the old man through the gate. When they were approaching the scene where the car got stuck, they were surprised to see about ten men waiting for them. "I told you I was going to arrange for the men to come," the old man boasted.

"Oh, my! Where will I get the money to pay them?" she exclaimed.

"Oh no, they don't ask for money."

"They will do it free for me?" Njeri asked in surprise.

They all shouted, "*Haraaambe!*" and responded to it, "*Twende!*"

The car was out of the mud in a split of a second. Njeri took the contacts of the old man, shook hands of the other men, thanked them for their support and entered her car.

"*Kwaheri mama, Mungu aende na wewe!*" the old man shouted, waving his hand.

"Aunt, now you know the direction?" Nelly asked, a pleasant tone in her voice.

"Yes, I know; the old man explained to me clearly."

"Shall we be driving for long?"

"Yes, half an hour at least."

"Oh, I am really tired and bored."

"I know. I am too. I hate driving long distances."

"Do you think we shall find Mummy has recovered?"

"Hopefully, let us wait till we reach there."

Nelly's skirt was crumpled. They had slept in their clothes and hadn't bothered to remove them. Their hair was wound up into sisal-like balls, and their faces still carried their night's sleep.

It was nine when they reached Namgoi. The market was a small one with a few scattered stooping stalls. They drove past the market and were now on another muddy road, but not so muddy as to get stuck again. Njeri drove carefully along, and speeded at some parts of the road. As they were approaching Cheperit they heard a noise. It must be a big crowd, Njeri thought. As they entered the town, they bumped into a huge group of youth singing *"Haki yetu! Haki yetu! Haki yetu!"* These were definitely ODM supporters. Njeri reached this crowd and found them struggling with the policemen. The latter were trying to prevent them from moving beyond the point where they were. One policeman approached Njeri's car, and bending low, signalled her to open the window. When she did, he said, *"mama, hapa si pazuri, utarudi."*

"Nirudi? Hapana, I can't go back," Njeri sounded defiant, and rude.

"Basi endesha pole pole," he gave in.

Njeri drove through the crowd as the policemen shielded her car from the unruly mob. But the youth, who were bitter and angry, attempted to lift the car wanting to topple it. Others stoned it and shattered all the glass windows, including the windscreen. Nelly screamed, but Njeri nestled her close to her side. "Don't be afraid, Nelly," she assured her. The policeman foiled the determination of one man who tried to deflate the right back tyre. When another man placed a log across the road before the car, one policeman ran in to remove it. As he removed it, other youth were lifting up the car and wanting to overturn it; others threw stones on it and dented its body. The policemen were overwhelmed and they had to shoot a tear gas canister in the air to disperse the crowd. *"Mama, enda sasa,"* one policeman said with a voice of urgency.

Njeri speeded up the road as the angry youth followed with stones and sticks. As she negotiated a corner she almost knocked down a goat, but quickly swerved to the left to avoid it. She looked back and the youth had given up; their stones could not reach their car. When she had driven about one kilometre from the scene of the rowdy youth, Njeri stopped the car and came out to see the damage. The windscreen and all glass windows had been shattered; its body was badly dented and its headlights all broken, leaving the electrical wires hanging out. The car was now a wreck. She was angry and bitter. She entered the vehicle and started driving at a crazy speed. In one hour they had reached Mosoriot.

They reached Eldoret at six in the evening. They attracted stares from passers-by, partly because of the dented car and partly because she was a woman driving during a volatile period. They headed straight to Eldoret District Hospital, which was situated in the suburbs. They enquired for a ward where patients with burns were treated. When they were taken there, a nurse on duty told them it was not time to see sick people, and that they had to wait up to eight o'clock. Njeri and Nelly parked the car in the hospital compound and had a stroll in town, window-shopping and looking at people. There was tension and restlessness in town. When it was eight o'clock, Njeri and Nelly went back to the hospital. The nurse on duty opened the door for them to get in. "Which patient do you want to see?" she asked them.

"Nyambura," Njeri said, and her mind started working on omens.

"Nyambura? Do we really have that name?" she asked herself, and didn't need a response.

"She has burns she sustained when her house was razed down by—" she explained.

"I am sure we don't have that name in this ward."

"Another name?"

"Kimani."

"No," she said with certainty. "When did she come?"

"I don't know, but it should be a couple of days ago."

"No, we don't have someone like that here."

Njeri was stranded and her mind went blank. Something came to her mind: Might Nyambura have succumbed to her injuries and taken to the mortuary? Yes, most probably.

"And where is the mortuary, maybe we could check there as well," she spoke and a tear formed in her eye. "Nyambura, my sister!" she heaved a sigh.

"Oh, yes. It could be that she passed on and was taken to the mortuary," the nurse explained.

"Go out of this hall and follow down the foot lane. The mortuary is at the end."

Njeri sighed. She held her heart. Nelly followed from behind. Nyambura is dead, she said to herself. When they were at the end of the lane, they went into a building which was obviously a mortuary going by the stench that wafted from inside. The receptionist was a thin emaciated woman in a red scarf. "Kindly, we are looking for Nyambura Kimani," she told her.

"Nyambura Kimani?" she asked absent-mindedly. "She bent down and pulled up a file. She opened and peered into it. She scanned down the list of names, turned a leaf and scanned again and flipped another and scanned from top to bottom. When she came to the last page she looked up and asked, "Nyambura Kemo?"

"No."

"Then we don't have Nyambura Kimani. She is not here," she said, closed the file, hurled it into the drawer below and looked away. Any more talk Njeri made fell on deaf ears. "But I have told you, such a name is not here," she shouted angrily.

Njeri and Nelly left the mortuary and drove to town. It was a half past nine. Despite the darkness, people were still staring at their car. They decided to drive to Bokima where Nyambura lived. It took them half an hour to reach there. Once in the Bokima shopping centre Njeri enquired for the home of the area chief. One old man, whom Njeri had to pay for his service, entered the car and led them to Chief Kipruto who lived on a hill. Good luck they found the chief at home. He welcomed them, and then asked where they had come from, and why the car was dented. Njeri told him all the tribulations of their journey from Nairobi. He then asked them why they wanted to see him. They asked him whether he knew someone by the name of Nyambura Kimani who contested as a councilor in Asegisegi ward on a PNU ticket. The chief's face revealed dread. He was tongue-tied, grew wrinkles on his forehead and sighed.

"Nyambura?" he asked again, curved his lower and upper lips and whistled, and shook his head for a long time, then finally, in a low solemn voice: "She died!" Njeri looked at him with an expressionless face. She stared at him, clutching the hem of her dress, and tears formed and dropped down her face. Nelly screamed, "Mummy is dead!" Njeri held her hand and nestled her. "Don't cry now. We shall know about it tomorrow."

It was now a half past ten o'clock, and the chief was still explaining and seemed to have much more to talk about Nyambura's death.

"Where are you intending to spend the night?"

"Nowhere in particular," Njeri said.

"You can spend the night with us here. Tomorrow in the morning we can walk to the graves." the chief explained.

Njeri cupped her two cheeks in the palms of her hands, as she walked into the chief's house. The family members had already caught word of who they were and were in the mood of sympathizing with them. The chief's wife was a portly lady with an inquisitive stare. Her two daughters were the quiet type. They busied themselves with washing dishes in the kitchen and preparing food for the following day's breakfast. The adjacent house to the living house was for the chief's daughters. There was one son, who was at the table, reading. Outside were numerous cows and goats.

That night Njeri didn't sleep a wink. She saw Nyambura's image throughout the night. She recalled all the things they did together as children, the school they attended, the day Nyambura was married and the day she divorced her abusive husband.

When morning came Njeri woke up with a sense of loss. Both took breakfast absent-mindedly, sobbing, wiping their faces from time to time. The chief's wife tried to comfort them but her words were not sufficient to bring an iota of hope or happiness to Njeri's heart.

"Can we drive in my car, even though it has no windows?"

"No, we can drive in mine," the chief said, but again quickly changed his mind. "Oh, I remember it doesn't have enough fuel."

"Then let us drive in mine, although a wreck."

They entered Njeri's car and drove into the forest. They crossed a valley and drove between tall trees. The road led into the bush where crosses protruded up. This was the cemetery. They came out of the car and solemnly walked along rows of graves, looking for the name on the blocks. They finally came to one written:

NYAMBURA KIMANI

DIED 30/12/2007

MAY GOD REST HER SOUL IN PEACE

Njeri placed some flowers on the gravestone and uttered a prayer. Nelly broke down beside her. It was early in the morning and the sun prolonged their shadows, making them look like vampires.

When Njeri lifted her eyes from the grave, she saw, to her horror, people hurrying down from a bushy hillside towards them. "Let us run!" the chief shouted. "Be quick, those people are coming to kill you, Njeri!" he looked frightened. "They are armed." Njeri's heart gave a dreadful leap and then, as dreadfully, seemed to have stopped forever. Before she could ask him to explain further, the chief had fled down the valley. Njeri was stranded. Nelly clung to her. The people had reached near her. The chief was already climbing up the other side of the valley. Njeri uttered a prayer and said to herself that she was ready to die if they wanted to kill her. The men, who reached her first, were reluctant to come close to her car. They did some gesture with their hands, pointing towards the bush yonder. Njeri could not understand what they meant, but she was now sure they had not come to harm anyone.

"*Chubot*, the cursed one, over there," the two men said and again pointed towards the bush. *"nyonba"*

One of them moved nearer and held her hand and Njeri allowed herself to be led towards the bush. They reached near the bush and Njeri heard a groaning sound, a shuffling of feet and a rustling of activities. She stood, panic-stricken. Nelly clung to her skirt.

One of the men went into the bush and came out with some old men and women who smiled at Njeri as a way of expressing their harmlessness to her. Njeri understood. She stooped her tall figure as she walked under the canopy of the dense bush. To her horror, she found almost a hundred people, all seated, and in the middle of them all was a man who wriggled senselessly on the ground in great pain, and from time to time gave an anguished shriek. Njeri pulled herself together and forced air into her lungs. "*Chubot*, the cursed one," the men said and pointed at him, and then turned towards

Njeri with merciful eyes. Njeri was shocked when the men asked her to touch his head so that he could come out of his condition.

"What for?" Njeri asked, looking at them for an answer.

One man walked up to her and stood close to her ear. "You know this man killed your sister, Nyambura."

"Killed my sister?" Njeri wailed, her voice dumbfounded, the sound coming from her mouth belonging to a stranger. She lowered her eyes down to the man. His bony figure was clad in a threadbare shirt that left a good part of his back uncovered. He tied his tattered long trousers with a rope. His fingernails were long and dirty, his eyes were red and cruel. She peered at him for a long time, engulfed in hatred, bitterness and antipathy. Lastly, when she recovered from the shocking revelation, she asked: "So, then, what does he want?" When Njeri asked this question, tears were already coursing down her cheeks. When the women in the crowd saw this, they lowered their heads and sobbed with her, pulling up their *lesos* to wipe their tears. "He is cursed," the man continued to explain. "Since he did the abominable thing he has never gone back to his family. Our custom does not allow him to go back home till he is pardoned." Now Njeri could understand what was happening and why the people gathered there. The man had stayed in the bush waiting to be cleansed, and the only person who could cleanse him was one related to the dead. They must have heard that Njeri had come and they made this impromptu meeting to cleanse their man.

The man tried to sit upright, but was unable; his body had grown weak, his skin was flaccid and his bones showed out. His hair was a big tuft of sisal on his head; he was disheveled and hungry. He looked frail and dying. The man tried for the second time to sit up, but fell down supine on the ground. He then sprawled his vein-lined arm on the ground and, with effort, lifted his torso a little up from the ground and managed to crawl towards Njeri. When he reached her, he nuzzled against her legs, uttering "*nyoiwon kat,* forgive me," and sobbed and bedewed her feet, legs, knees, and skirt, with his tears.

"The man has been waiting for you for the last two weeks," the man standing next to Njeri explained, influencing her feeling further.

"He is my husband," a woman's voice came from the multitude. Then Njeri saw a woman breaking down amidst the crowd. They held her, as she tore at her clothes, and pulled her hair. The pain of losing a husband, Njeri thought. "Please forgive him. I need him back home!" the woman shouted and screamed, a number of strong men tried to contain her.

"Put your hands on his head and he will be pardoned," a pleading voice came from the crowd.

"Pardon my brother," said the man who was standing one meter away from Njeri. It was the brother of the dying man. The dying man held Njeri's legs tightly and looked up at her, waiting to be forgiven.

Njeri looked down at him and then swept her eyes over the anxious faces, and felt something melting in her, and that something flowed in her body, down to the man. It was her innermost feeling. Her heart gave way. She saw between her and the people, and the man, and the human race, a divine hand, which bonded them together as a human race. Beings created by one God. She felt in her a boiling sensation, a feeling of humanity, a feeling that we are all mortals and one day we shall all die, and the only thing we own in the world is love for our fellow human beings; and the only time we have it for them is when we are still alive; when we die we never have a chance to love and forgive. She placed her hands upon the man's head. "I forgive you, *Chubot*, the cursed one!" Immediately her words were followed by a chanting from among the people. Njeri guessed the chant was a thanksgiving to her and to God.

When Njeri left the place and walked towards her car she felt relieved that she had forgiven someone in bondage. Before she could open the door of her car, she saw a crowd of policemen running towards her direction, the chief among them. She was shocked. She stood still, her mouth agape. When they reached her, the chief who was panting asked, "Have they harmed you?"

"Oh, no," Njeri replied.

"What was it then?" the chief asked.

"Why did they want you?" the policemen enquired.

"*Chubot*," Njeri said and pointed towards the bush, and was lost for words.

The Beautiful Red Bag

It was evening and the sun had buried its flame in the horizon. Sarange hurried home from school. The day had been a happy one. It was the end of the term and she had come top of her class in the end of the year exam. She was called to the front of the school and everyone was asked to clap for her. Her class teacher awarded her a beautiful red bag. The children and teachers clapped and cheered her as she unzipped the bag, revealing some other prizes. There was a brown geometrical set, a ruler and a notebook. Her class teacher promised to buy her a new school uniform the following year when she went to standard seven. She was delighted and she came home bubbling with joy and pride. She would pass her KCPE exam in standard eight, she thought. She will then go to Alliance Girls and later join the University of Nairobi. She would attain her degree in medicine and become a doctor, she mused. She was determined to excel. She was going to work harder than she had done before in order to realize her dreams.

She came through the gate that stood on the fence encircling their homestead. As she walked across the vast compound, she felt a warm sensation of joy sweeping down her back. Her father was going to be surprised to see her beautiful red bag and the rest of the prizes. Her mother would be overwhelmed with bliss and ecstasy. The entire village was going to hear about her success and will share in her happiness. Her friends at home who went to other schools will be jealous of her prizes. She was simply going to be the talk of the village for a couple of weeks to come.

As she crossed the bare ground outside the main house, she was startled by her father's deep voice. "Sarange come back here!" he shouted. "This here is your visitor." Sarange quickly looked to her left and saw, standing at the cowshed beside the house, her father. Beside him was a burly, pot-bellied old man whose beard was ragged and bushy, and whose forehead was long, wrinkled and exceeded onto his balding head, giving him a fierce cast of expression that would strike fear into any body. Sarange stood still, transfixed, shocked at the unusual approach of her father. "Come on and greet him. Be quick!" Sarange found herself scurrying towards them, confused, filled with suspicion and foreboding. When she reached the two men, her father asked her to shake the visitor's hand which she did with a bow of her body. "Go into the house now and prepare yourself thoroughly. You are going out for a long journey."

Without comprehending the meaning of her father's words, Sarange turned to go. She could not have questioned. He was not the sort of man to be asked questions. His word was gospel and was final. He loathed women who stood before him asking questions, or demanding clarifications. His lips trembled with rage before such women and would most likely be tempted to drive sense into them. Sarange left the two men and squirmed into the house. She then took the geometrical set and note book out of her new beautiful red bag and

carried them on her hand. The prizes were to catch her mother's attention. She found her mother seated at the fireplace, her head cupped in her palms. "Mummy, look, my red bag," Sarange spoke with pride, as she moved close to her mother. Her mother didn't move. Sarange realized that she was sobbing. She stood still, peering at her with astonishment and bewilderment. She could not comprehend all that was happening. Her father spoke of a long journey—what journey was it? Her mother crying at the fireplace—what had happened to her? She was perturbed. She was almost in tears herself.

"Go to your hut and dress up, Sarange," her mother said, raised her head from her lap and wiped tears from her eyes. "You are going on a journey."

"What do you mean, Mother?"

"You are going to another place."

"Another school, Mother?"

"Be it school or not, you are going away?"

"What do you mean, Mother?"

"A journey, to which I, your mother, have no power to say no."

"To Grandma, Mother?"

"To Grandma, or not, it is a journey. "

"But Mother— "

"Go prepare yourself. Don't ask questions. You are now a grown up and should understand all that is happening."

"But Mother—"

"Don't waste time. Go and prepare yourself. You know your father very well. He will blow up his tops if he finds you here. It is not my wish that this should happen."

Sarange put back her prizes into her bag, disappointed, and went out. She entered her hut, filled with uneasiness and uncertainty. She put on her Sunday red skirt and a white striped blouse. She put on her blue pair of socks and her black school shoes. She then packed in an old polythene paper bag, her pullover, one extra dress, a pair of slippers and two underpants. Her new beautiful red schoolbag was to carry only her prizes, she thought. The prizes will come in handy in case her parents were taking her to a new school. She had heard of boarding schools where children were taken to learn and they slept and ate there without coming home. These schools were like their homes. It would be exciting if she was taken to one of those schools. She would then show her prizes to other pupils and prove to them her prowess in class.

It was coming to nightfall and more men had joined her father and the old grey-bearded visitor at the cowshed. It had grown into a small crowd of men and women who were talking in subdued voices, with a mixture of happiness and anxiety written all over their faces. Sarange watched them through the wooden window of the main hut and wondered why they were all there and what they were up to. Apprehension and dread grew bigger and bigger in her, but was, from time to time, broken by the exhilarating thought of her beautiful red bag and the immense pride that it brought into her heart.

It was now dark and the birds had long quietened in their nests. Cows and goats had been penned in their enclosure and little hustles and bustles went on in the neighbourhood. Sarange, carrying a small bundle of clothes in polythene on one shoulder and the beautiful red bag containing her prizes, on the other, was escorted out of her father's compound by people who were largely strangers. Quiet among this company were her mother and father. There were also her aunt and few village women with whom she was familiar.

They walked through a forest that had a thick canopy of foliage above their heads that spread wide and far like the roof of a house. Sarange felt awkward, walking among the silent crowd. She walked close to her mother, clutching at her skirt and feeling her waist belt. "Are we about to arrive, Mummy?" she whispered up at her mother. Her mother kept quiet. "Is it a school Mummy?"

her mother kept quiet. "Shall we go to our Grandma's place?" Her mother nudged her. She gave up asking questions. The path now narrowed, leading into thick undergrowths that were covered with dew. Sarange's shoes were wet and she realized she had become numb on the toes and ankles, and was starting to shiver.

The procession came down a small valley, paved with rocks on either side. This led them to a swelling river. "We used to swim here," Sarange thought to herself. That was long time ago when she was in standard three. They crossed a wide bridge made from thick timbers and oak trees. Sarange held the wooden handrails and felt a pleasant sensation that the night brought in her heart. On the other side of the river Sarange noticed scattered bushes and tall grass covered in the moonlit night, through which they walked in silence. Sarange looked up at the sky and saw the half moon whose light was lighting the vast field where they walked.

They had walked for one hour when the procession suddenly stopped. Sarange breathed a sigh of relief. The old grey-bearded, pot-bellied man pushed forward and led them into a gate made of old corrugated iron sheets. They entered in a single file. They were now in a huge compound that was lit by the moonlight. Sarange realized that the compound was filled with murmuring, which grew into audible conversations and which finally burst into ululations, song and dance. Sarange became aware of the many people in the compound, who must have been waiting for them. She also noticed that every one took interest in her and shook her hand with a gesture of familiarity. Sarange listened to their song and she heard her name in the words. They referred to her name, adorning it with praise and admiration. She was puzzled. She did not understand why. How did they know her name? Who told them? She listened to the words of the song, but utterly failed to make head or tail of them.

"Sarange, the beautiful one!" the soloist sang.

"Sarange, the mother of this village!" the others answered in a chorus.

"Sarange, the wanted one, now found!" the soloist said, high-pitchedly.

"Sarange, the mother of this village!"

"Sarange, the God-send!"

"Sarange the mother of this village!"

This song brought reminisces of closing day ceremony when children and teachers sung her a song of compliment and congratulation: "Good girl, Good girl! Try again! Try again another time!" They had sung praises and paeans in honour of her name as she received her prizes, as she shook the hands of her teachers and as she, during her small speech to the school, spoke one point after another. Like those pupils and teachers at her school, these people, too, were happy for her. They showed intimacy and curiosity in her. But why were they happy, she wondered. Why were they dancing? Her name.... well, her name, what was it for?...why her name and not someone else's?... Her parents..... so silent....so mysteriously quiet.......no one attempted to explain anything. Is there a school here?.....No. This had nothing to do with school. It was just an occasion of some sort—a village wedding, an ordinary village gathering, or just a stop-over to some destinations. But what meaning had it?....She was puzzled.

She was shown a hut that stood on the left, at the far end corner of the compound. Sarange, in the procession, entered in this hut that was dimly lit with a can lamp. Sarange saw beer in pots, milk in guards and honey in plates. They all sat down on lower stools and drank. Sarange was given honey and milk to feed on. It had been a good journey and an exciting visit, Sarange thought, as she ate the honey and then joined in the songs sang by the old women in the hut.

"Sarange, the God-send!" the soloist started.

"The mother of this village!" the women replied.

"Sarange, the wanted one. Now found!"

"The mother of this village!" they chorused.

"Sarange, the beautiful one!"

"The mother of this village!"

As the song went on, Sarange noticed the movement in and out of the hut. Women and men came in, drank and left, while others reclined their bodies against the clay wall of the hut. When it was midnight, Sarange realized that she was alone among the strangers. Her people had long gone back to their home during the night. The strangers also left shortly afterwards and she was left with the old grey-bearded, pot-bellied man. She was filled with distrust and dubiousness. Sarange finally realized the trick. She had been duped. It dawned on her that this was going to be her husband. She was going to be his wife. She had heard such arrangements happening to other girls of her age before and she never, at any one time, thought that this could happen to her. She realized she had been trapped and had no way out of it. She knew it was the end of the road for her. She froze on the three-legged stool on which she sat. Her heart palpitated and pounded in her like a roll of drums. She felt tense and nervous. She clutched her beautiful red bag as a way of consolation. She took out her geometrical set and opened it, examining the protractor, the set square and the rubber. She recalled the ceremony on the closing day with all its merriment. Her new beautiful red bag…will it ever see the school in which it was given? No! Her classmates and teachers…will they ever see her again? Oh, no! Where will the class teacher take the school uniform he promised to buy for her the following year? Her dream of becoming a doctor…. would it ever be realized? No, no! She would be a house wife, and no one will ever know that she one time topped her class. The train of her thoughts stung her eyes and tears beaded in her eyeballs.

The dim light of the can-lamp drew a long shadow on the clay wall opposite. Sarange looked up. The old man carried his pot-bellied body across towards her. "Feel welcome, Sarange," the man broke the silence, smoothed his long ragged beard and nodded his balding head. "This now is your house to live in, to keep and to cherish."

Sarange wanted to tell him off, but she couldn't speak. She took in a deep breath, and let the air out nervously. It was fear. She held back her tears by burying her head in her lap. Without further communication the old man paced up and down the house putting things in place. He tried to take away Sarange's polythene luggage and the beautiful red bag, but Sarange held onto them tightly and refused to let them go. He gave up and went into the bedroom where he spent a few minutes before coming out. When he finally emerged, the man tried to make advances to Sarange, but was met with a rude shock. Sarange coiled her little body on the stool and refused to move. The man gave up and sat on a chair near the table.

"This is your home, Sarange. It is your house and be ready to take it, live in it and be happy." Sarange shook her shoulders in protest. Tears choked her. "You are now my wife, remember; and I am here to take care of you." Sarange blew her nose and wiped her tears. "I paid dowry for you three years ago, you hear?" Sarange kept quiet. Tears coursed down her tender cheeks. "I will make you happy, Sarange."

The man stood up, came towards Sarange for the second time. He shook up her thin fragile shoulders. She shrugged him off, pushing away his wrinkled clammy hands. "Come on," the man spoke in a deep voice, grabbed her thin wrist and lifted her up. She was filled with dread.

"Stop holding me like that," Sarange barked in anger, wringing her wrist from him.

"You are not a child anymore, you hear?" he thundered. "You are a wife. Understand?"

"Me? Your wife?" She pushed him off.

He came down upon her with renewed energy. He grabbed Sarange's torso. When he tried to drag her to the bedroom, she elbowed him on the belly and the man jerked back, and Sarange took the opportunity and freed herself and, with her beautiful red bag, quickly darted out through the open door and disappeared into the dark night. The man followed behind in hot pursuit and caught up with her outside at the banana plantation. As he pushed her in, bubbling with rage and fury, he grabbed away her beautiful red bag and hurled it violently upon her youthful tender face. It hit her eyes and dropped to the floor and the prizes slipped out, scattering on the floor.

"My beautiful red bag! Oh! Oh! Oh my bag!" she cried so loudly, beads of tears rolling down her cheeks, as she collected the scattered items and putting them into her red bag. She stood up, heaving and gasping for air, mucus and tears streaming down her cheeks.

"If you continue behaving like this, I am going to beat sense into this little head," he warned in acid tones. Sarange, clutching onto her red bag, sat down on a three-legged stool and, at one time, seemed to resign to her fate. When the old man had calmed down, Sarange suddenly came onto her feet and, with all the energy her legs could summon, flew out of the house again; but before she could thrust into the darkness and disappear, the old man's vein-lined long hands grabbed her, carried her on his shoulder and brought her once again into the house. He wrung the red bag from her hands and flogged her small head with it once again. The strap of the bag tore off and the piece fell on the floor. "My red bag! My red bag is torn! Torn!" Sarange screamed hysterically as if her own life had been torn. She picked the piece of

strap from the floor and clasped it tightly in her hand, like someone holding her piece of life.

The man, heaving with fury, took her by the scrap of her neck. "Little girl" he shouted, anger shading his voice. He slapped her on the face, a slap that saw her reel down onto the bumpy floor. Dizzy and almost unconscious, she crawled on her belly and took cover under the table. The old man bent down and picked her by the skirt. "Stupid. Is this the way you are going to behave as a wife?" he spoke with fury, dragging her out. Sarange was screaming, but nobody came to her help. The man's elderly wives could not be expected to come to her rescue as this was the same experience they had to undergo before they fully became wives. The neighbours, too, could not intervene since wife-beating was the norm in the village.

As he dragged her little body on the earthen floor, Sarange suddenly remembered her only weapon she could bring into use to avert the violence meted out upon her. She had learned it from her late grandmother during sessions she held with Sarange in which she taught her the common taboos of her people: Sarange struggled to come on to her feet, and when she managed, she swung back one step, then quickly gathered the hem of her skirt and pulled it up to her waist, baring her haunches and unveiling her pants. The man froze on the spot. He stared at Sarange's tender legs and thighs and was struck with shock. As if that was not enough for the old man's eyes, Sarange pulled down her pants, exposing her pudenda and pubic hair. She held the pants tightly in her hand. He stared at her, not believing his eyes. What was she up to, the man wondered. Had she given in and now wanted him for the night? Looking at the figure before him, the man's muscles twitched. His flesh became tense and hard. He bit his lips, drooled on the mouth and saliva escaped at the corner of his mouth. While the man was dazed with shock and lust, Sarange suddenly jumped forward and landed at him, raised the pants above her head and—God forbid!-- lashed him with it. It was all over.... The man was finished.... The act was irreversible. The man stood, transfixed like a ghost. He stood there as if he had been struck by lightning. It was taboo for a woman to beat a man with her own underwear.

The man stood, dump founded. He then suddenly burst out into a scream like an animal in terrible pain. He shouted, "curse! Curse! Curse!" until the word rattled off the walls like stone-shot. He knew it was all over. Sarange was not going to be his wife according to tradition. He had lost a wife. He wished he had taken more caution. He screamed so loudly that his first and second wives who had been quietly following the proceedings from a safe distance at the windows of their huts, came running in. Neighbours, too, who were eavesdropping from far away behind the fences and from their huts, ran in and thronged outside the hut. Taboo had been committed. Beating a man with a pant was abominable. Sarange was going to be the first woman to commit such an offence, at least in the recent times. It was going to cost seven bulls and seven white hens to avert the bad omen likely to be caused by Sarange's action. The seven bulls and the seven hens would be slaughtered at Sarange's home, after which the marriage will be terminated. The animals' blood would be sprinkled on the ground outside Sarange's hut to appease the ancestral spirits to cleanse her abominable act. The heads, limbs, skins and entrails would be thrown in the forest to appease the gods of fertility and this would avert the calamity likely to befall the old man for the curse contracted from the woman's pant. The man had lost a wife for whom he had waited patiently over the years. Having paid dowry for her three years earlier while she was in standard three, the man was sure to own her as a wife. He now could not believe having lost her.

The village people who congregated in the homestead were tongue-tied. They bent their heads low and kept mum. It was gloomy and grave. Sarange watched them, examined their faces and felt like laughing out loud. She knew she had escaped it. "Well done! Well done! Try again! Try again! Good girl!" she whispered the song to herself. She clutched her red beautiful bag and the prizes and held them close to her side. She kept the piece of strap that broke from the bag, so carefully as if she was keeping her own life. She was bubbling with happiness; her heart vibrated with excitement. When the slaughtering of the goats and hens are done, she thought, she would be free to go to school the following year.

Let It Live

Nerima sat on the bench waiting to get in. There were five patients to go before her turn came. Something strange seems to have been happening to her body; something that disrupted her monthly cycle. She had not 'seen' her monthly period for three months now, and she was worried. She wanted to be sure she was not pregnant. She was disturbed and had not slept a wink the previous nights. She was only in form three, and had one more year to go before she completed her secondary school. If she was pregnant it would be the end of the road for her. She would drop out of school and never realize her dreams.

One more patient was called in. There were four more now remaining: three men and one pregnant woman who sat next to her. The pregnant woman looked weak and emaciated. Her lips were dry and her eyes were sunken. Behind Nerima was a long queue of about twenty patients, women and men. Nerima looked around and noticed that some of the women were pregnant, and some had recently given birth and had their little ones with them. The woman next to Nerima was fondling and kissing her small baby boy, who was handsome and playful. The kid kept smiling at Nerima, grabbing at her dress and tousling her hair.

The pregnant woman in front of her suddenly started groaning in pain. She attracted people's attention and they all looked in her direction. She leaned against the wall, with her limbs straggling on the bench. Shortly she started foaming at the corner of her mouth, and leant her body on Nerima. Shocked, Nerima held her up and looked around for help. The nurses on duty noticed, rushed out and quickly took her away. Pregnancy was a painful experience, Nerima thought. The image of the pregnant woman remained in her mind for a little while. If Nerima's test results were positive, she didn't know what she would do. She would probably never let the pregnancy advance, but take Chloroquin tablets and have the little nestling intoxicated, its wings and limbs stunted and its breath stifled. The little thing will never see the light of day, she thought. She would be a fresh girl again, free of stigma and the admonition of parents, teachers and friends. She would walk around freely as though nothing had happened, and this would give her a chance to redesign her life. She then would be more cautious, more thoughtful and prudent. I will never let the pregnancy mature, she thought. After all, is there a man in the world who would marry a lady with a kid? No man in his right mind would do that. Then why should a lady subject herself to such a rejection? Why accept to be a mother when you know that no man would marry you?

Another patient was called in. There were three to go before Nerima. The little boy behind her pulled at her hair. Nerima turned and felt her pony-tail between her fingers, and smiled at the boy.

"He is naughty. Sorry," his mother apologized to Nerima.

"Never mind," Nerima said, smiling and looking in the woman's direction.

"Are you a parent?" the woman asked in a friendly tone.

"No, not yet," answered Nerima. "Why are you asking?"

"Someone who is not a parent will find it irritating."

"I know," Nerima said and smiled, blushing. "But with me, I do understand." She waved her hand at the child. "*Ti-ti-ti-ti*." The child grabbed one of her fingers and pulled it into his small mouth. He clawed it between his teeth for a little while. Nerima felt embarrassed, but she put on a smiling face to show that everything was alright. She looked at the boy and thought he was handsome. What a handsome boy! She exclaimed to herself. Children are God's gift, she thought, and they are blessings to mankind.

The child released her finger, still smiling at her as if he knew the effect it had on Nerima. The mother of the boy laughed. "I told you he is naughty. So naughty." She then pinched his cheeks.

"Never mind," said Nerima. "One day I will also have one like him," she said and the words weighed heavily upon her own mind. I will be happy to become a mother, she thought to herself. "How old is he?"

"Two, going three."

"To have a child is a blessing," Nerima said.

"Oh, yeah, a big blessing! Plan and have one soon," she said and laughed to herself. "It is a blessing to see your own image," she laughed again, threw the boy into the air and held him down onto her lap. Nerima was absorbed in deep thought. The woman's words sunk into her mind and lodged there. A blessing... it is a blessing... to see your own image, your image...image...image....

"Sure?" Nerima said absentmindedly. Unconsciously, she passed her hand under her belly and pressed hard on the little swelling that was developing there. Another patient was called in. There were two remaining before Nerima's turn came.

"I gave birth to this boy before I was married," the woman went on, smiling and blushing. "His biological father denied responsibility."

"Really?" Nerima spoke, her voice tinged with shock. "You didn't think of aborting?"

"Oh no!" the woman cried. "Why should I kill an innocent child?"

"So did you get married later?"

"Of course, I am now married. Not to his biological father."

"You mean his father never came back to you?"

"He did, but it was too late. I was already married. In any case I wouldn't have accepted him back after he walked out on me."

"Oh, happy to hear that you could not abort."

"You don't abort, you let it live. God has reasons why He lets things happen."

"Oh yes," Nerima nodded her head, steeped in the conversation. She looked at the woman and the child and marvelled. She was not going to be the first one, she thought, there were many in the world. Her parents will understand. She will narrate the whole incident to her mother and she was sure she would empathize with her. She will then inform her father of her situation. The school principal was also a very understanding lady. In the past she had assisted many girls at her school who fell into a similar trap. She allowed them continue with classes while they breastfed their children at their homes. Some could not return to her school because of the stigma, and she made arrangements for them to transfer to other schools where they completed their secondary education. She was motherly and full of empathy.

The patient in front of her was called in. Nerima was now the next one on the queue. She held her breath. She had given a sample of her urine in the laboratory and the result had been forwarded to the doctor in this room to which she was going. What might be the results? Positive or negative? She wondered. Agony twisted in her. Premonition and death both dragged at her like a ball and chain. Did life bear any meaning? Why do we live and suffer such torments and pain? Is life of any purpose? She examined her future, the future for which she had worked so hard, and she saw it--broad and expansive like the sky--covered in a wide sheet of darkness.

Suppose she was pregnant, she asked herself again. Her mind went blank. And the blank space was slowly filled up by images of her father: old unkempt man, with tattered trousers, shirt and shoes, labouring so hard in the farm to see her go to school. What will happen when he learns about her condition? Will he overcome the shock of the terrible news?.... No! Not at all. Maybe her decision to "let live" will bring her more disgrace than the blessings of which the woman with the child delightedly spoke. Giving birth will be suicidal. It would stain her forever and, with the kid around and growing, she would never recover from such torment. The best thing is to flush it out once she confirms it is there. No one will know she ever did it. She will be a free woman once again......

Her well-formed train of thoughts suddenly got blurred, became amorphous and indistinct and then, as if from a distant world, a voice gently called upon her: "Mother! Mother! Spare me! Spare me mother!" The voice whimpered upon her mind repeatedly, consistently and persistently, until she, the mother, turned inside into herself and saw, in her mind's eye, her own child dying, and as life exuded out of it, it pleaded for a chance to live; it moaned and cursed so much that Nerima suddenly turned, as if startled from a deep sleep, to look behind her--accidentally she caught the hand of the little boy who was out again for his mischief. "I Love you my boy," she said, absentmindedly, in a moaning voice--and actually moaned.

Her name came floating through the narrow door, startling her from her train of thoughts. She stood up, shivering, bewildered and confused. She tottered through the narrow opening and entered the semi-dark room. At the far end corner, seated at a table, in a white overall, was a doctor. She trundled across the small room like someone carrying a heavy load on her head. She sat down and her mind went blank. He turned round to pick a sample of urine from the table behind him, and Nerima felt it was a hundred years before he turned round again to place it on the table. Her heart beat rapidly in her. She took in a deep breath and let it out noisily.

The doctor placed the bottle on the table and examined the result attached to it. He took centuries to read through the few lines on the piece of paper. Nerima moved, fidgeted, scratched her hands, twirled her thumbs, adjusting her thin body on the chair; the doctor's eyes were distracted and looked up, catching her legs swinging. She was embarrassed and almost broke down in tears. The doctor then took in a deep breath and an expression of pity formed on his face. Nerima watched all this and resigned to her fate.

"Which school do you go?" he asked at long last.

"St. Teresa's Girls," she found the words.

"Which form are you in now?" he asked, with a voice of concern.

"Three," she said and wanted to scream. She wanted to stop him from asking any more questions. He turned round again, this time searching for nothing. He looked disturbed. He turned to face her.

"Your pregnancy test...," he started, then stopped. Nerima's intestines coiled into one big lump inside her stomach. She saw in her mind's eye her father and mother, her school principal, her classmates, friends...............

"your pregnancy test came out--" the doctor continued, interrupting Nerima's train of thoughts "positive!"

"Positive?" the word echoed in her mind.

"You are pregnant, Nerima." The walls of the small room swayed before her. The chair on which she sat moved. She saw darkness descend upon her, and every door into her future was covered in that darkness. She froze on the chair. Her body was heavy to carry out, and when she managed to carry it she went away without a word. She walked out of the building, paced past the flower garden and crossed the car park. Once at the bus stop, she came to an abrupt stop. Then she felt, or imagined, her baby kicking, turning and bouncing inside her. With lively fingers, she clutched her belly, feeling the baby kick and turn. "Kick gently baby," she whispered to herself. "Turn gently baby, your mother is listening." She then caught herself smiling, pride and blithe playing in her heart. "When you come to this world, baby, I will be here to meet you..." She looked up and saw a bus coming. When it came to a halt she boarded it and left for home, determined to see her parents and the school principal.

The Machete's Cut

It was night and Lekishon's children were preparing supper after a long day spent at the farm. "It is time," Lekishon's lips moved to speak the words, as he gestured at his wife. "Let us be off." The wife followed the old man through the door. In his hand he carried a machete.

They stealthily walked through their dark homestead and crossed the fence that separated their home from that one of their neighbour, Kituku. They walked down towards the river on Kituku's farm. "See how rich this man is," Lekishon whispered to his wife, "He owns so much when we have nothing," he whispered, bitterness in his voice. "He won't feel it even if we took half what he owns."

"To steal from such a rich man is not a sin, is it?" his wife asked.

"It is not. God only condemns those who steal from the poor," he slashed the night with his machete, as if to justify to God of his reason to steal.

"Speak softly. Kituku's houses are nearby here," she whispered.

"I will only swing the machete once and the bunch will come down," he whispered into her ear.

"Hope the action won't cause noise," his wife whispered. "The people are still awake."

"You will place yourself below the plank. The bunch will fall on your head and we shall leave immediately."

"Swing once."

"Sure. I will swing this machete once and it will cut the thick plank into two. The bunch will be on your head."

They searched through the dark plantation and came to a group of banana bunches that were huge. The old man pointed at one of them. He then moved backwards from the plank and examined it up down in its outline against the moonlight. He looked down and, with his feet, trampled the tall grass on which he was standing to give himself a clear space for his swinging action as he cuts the plank. He was careful not to make an iota of

noise. The wife positioned herself below the big bunch of banana and raised her hands up, ready to hold it when it came, and walk away immediately she clutched it.

Lekishon swung back. "*Chwaa!*" the machete went. The bunch dropped onto his wife's head as expected. She clutched it, stood still for a while to assess the amount of noise the cutting action had made, and then she turned to go, followed by Lekishon. "Quick! Be quick!" he whispered.

"It seems the machete's tip touched my neck slightly, Lekishon."

"What? The tip?"

"Yes, the tip of the machete."

"Your neck?"

"Yes, my neck."

"You must have stood too close to me," he blamed her, breathing heavily.

"You swung the machete too far wide and touched me with it," she continued complaining silently, much to the chagrin of Lekishon.

"Quiet! Be quiet!"

"My neck! My neck, Lekishon!"

"Keep quiet! Let us keep going!"

"My neck. The machete's cut!"

"Quiet! People might hear us!"

"My neck! My neck! My neck!"

"Keep quiet, be quiet, we are about to reach home and we shall nurse the wound!"

"Oh, my neck!" she whispered as she panted under the heavy bunch of the banana.

They finally reached the fence that separated their homestead from their neighbour's. They squeezed through it and headed straight to their house. She was panting as she crossed the threshold into the house. Upon reaching the sitting room, she immediately threw down the heavy bunch of banana and asked for water to drink. She swilled the cold water and placed the cup on the table and asked for her sleeping mat. She threw herself on it to rest. She was heaving and sweating. Lekishon went into the kitchen to see what the children had prepared. As he came back to the sitting room, to his shock, he saw a big long snake unwinding itself from the bunch of bananas. He ran out, shouting: "Help! Help! Snake! Snake!" The children who were in the kitchen flew through the wooden window of the house and gathered outside to watch the enormous beast that coiled and raised its head to charge. They held their breath, and peered at it as their father shouted for help. The neighbours heard the commotion and ran in to see what was going on. Kituku was the first one to arrive with his machete and club.

"Good neighbours!" he panted. "Where is the snake?" he asked, heaving with anxiety.

"There!" Lekishon pointed. "It has emerged from the bunch of bananas."

Neigbours gathered and watched with fear and fright. The beast made a jerking movement at the threshold of the house, as a comedian does when he is sure he has captured the attention of his audience. The young men who were present collected sticks and stones which they threw at him. It became more aggressive as stones and sticks fell on its head. Each time it swung its neck up to the air, the women made sudden steps backwards, crying with dread. As more stones fell on it, it wriggled and coiled its enormous body in circles. It shook its tail rapidly and then rested it upon its body. It had died. One man came forward, turned its long torso over, and counted the white strips that ringed its neck. "Twenty years old," he concluded. "Very poisonous, indeed."

The great drama was over. Noise had also subsided, and children were now courageous enough to go into the house. They went straight to their mother who lay silently on her mat. Her lips had turned blue and her limbs twitched and moved. She was dead.

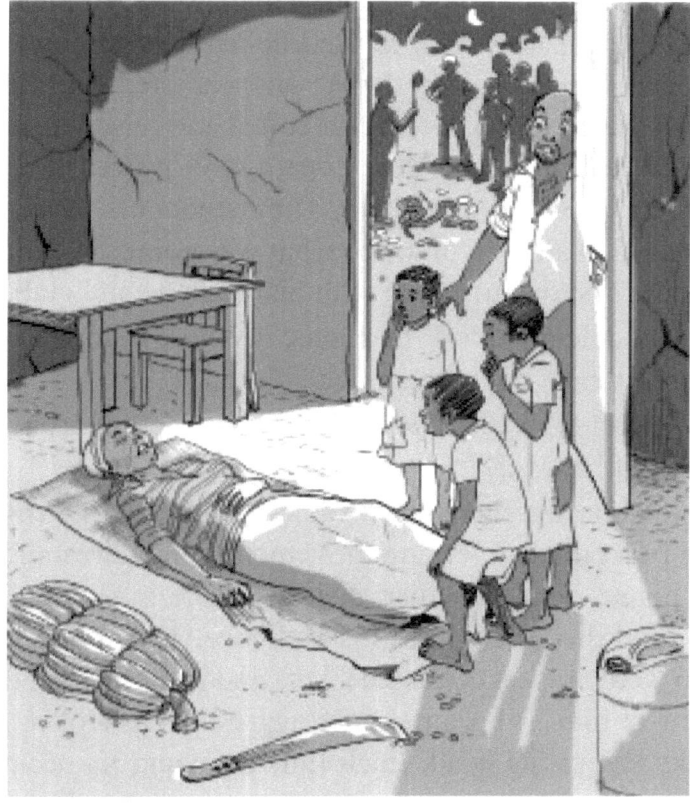

Nkatha's Changing Fortunes

The graduation ceremony was conducted outside on the college's vast field. The graduancs, clad in grey suits and red neck-ties, sat on chairs arranged in rows, with their guardians next to them. Nkatha sat on the front row, her Aunt on her left and Mogambi on her right. The little baby nestled comfortably on her lap. Nkatha looked behind her and she saw a sea of people. So many had turned up to attend their graduation ceremony. The principal, the tutors and various guests sat on the podium.

"Testing! Testing!" the Master of Ceremonies' voice flooded the air. The ceremony had begun. After prayer and the national anthem, the Master of Ceremonies introduced the tutors and the guests. Then she started calling names of graduands, one by one, and requesting them to go to the podium where each one was crowned with a wreath of flowers and issued with a certificate.

After ten students fetched their certificates, Nkatha knew her turn was soon coming. She bent her head to look at her baby. "Suckle quickly," she whispered down at him. "Don't you know today is a great day for your mother to be recognized as a teacher?" she thought. The baby started suckling ravenously. "Tik, tik tik tik" she teased him, pinching his cheeks and caressing his smooth hair.

As the boy suckled, she adjusted her suit and necktie and, bending down, pulled her socks up. She took in a deep breath and let it out with relief. At last the day had come! The day she had waited for such a long time. The two years had been bumpy, challenging and full of difficult times. She looked onto her right and met with Mogambi's eyes. He sat there quietly, sheepishly, quite unlike the old Mogambi she knew. Nkatha wanted to shout, "shame!" to his face, but instead murmured the word inside her heart. She felt a lump building in her throat and forcing tears to ooze in her eyes. This Mogambi, she thought…a devil… a devil, yes a devil. ... She felt like screaming at him, pulling at his clothes and, with her teeth, tearing his flesh into shreds. Mogambi was one person who had contributed immensely to her misery during her college life. She operated from her uncle's home during her college course, having been taken there after her parents died in a road accident. She recalled one evening when she urgently went to see Mogambi at his house. She started on this light note: "Mogambi, do you love me?"

"Of course. Why?" he asked with suspicion.

"You do? That is all I want to know," she said in a voice loaded with irony.

"Yes, I do."

"You know," she started, paced up and down the room, and when she brought herself down on a chair, she told Mogambi: "You know I am pregnant, Mogambi. I am carrying your baby."

"What?" This was a bomb that shook the chair on which he sat. He looked at Nkatha, confused. "What do you mean, Nkatha?"

"That is what I mean. Is it wrong to carry your baby?" she asked.

"How sure can I be it is my baby? It can be somebody else's"

"Somebody else's? Is that what you've got to say?"

"Yes. It can be somebody else's," he spoke with defiance. "Furthermore, why did you decide to conceive?"

"But it is you who did it," she cried out. "I had warned you, Mogambi, but you never heeded my pleas. I had warned you, didn't I?"

It is true she had warned him. That was three months earlier when she had come to visit him, and she happened to spend a night in his house. Mogambi, that night, without taking effort to control himself, let things happen. He went on the rampage and without restraint or an iota of qualms, sowed his wild oats upon Nkatha's innocence and naivety.

Nkatha's train of thoughts was interrupted. Her name had been called. "Nkatha!" her Aunt startled her, "your name! your name Nkatha! Go! Go!" She jumped up, and hurriedly perched the baby on her Aunt's lap. Immediately the baby burst into a scream. She grabbed him and threw him in Mogambi's lap, but the baby clung back onto Nkatha's coat so tightly that she could not detach him from her. She grabbed him up onto her bosom and hurried off with him to the podium. She shook the hands of the guests and went to the master of ceremonies who gave her a bunch of flowers and a certificate. Immediately the baby grabbed the flowers and pulled off the petals, sending the guests and students into fits of laughter. Nkatha smiled sheepishly, squirming, and covered her face as she walked back to her seat.

"He doesn't like anyone," her Aunt spoke in matter-of-fact way.

"He is used to staying with his mother," Mogambi laboured to explain the obvious, "that is why he is not used to being handled by other people."

Nkatha sat looking at her certificate. At long last she had graduated. She was going to be a teacher and get a salary. Her poverty, misery and what-not, had come to an end. She had become a member of a salaried class. She would be able to take care of her baby, bring him up well and see him grow to become a successful man. She will begin a part-time degree course at the University of Nairobi and will be attending classes during school holidays. With a job nothing was going to stop her. The sky was the limit. She unbuttoned her blouse and breastfed her baby. "Little baby! Ti-ti-ti" she teased him. He was a lovely baby, handsome and full of life. His future was bright, she thought. She recalled the night when she came from Mogambi's house after he rejected her. She had gone back to her uncle's house where she lived in the city and went straight to bed. She had wanted to terminate the pregnancy and smash the life of the little one nestling in her womb. She had tried with malariaquine, but that failed. She took the kitchen knife and wanted to end all her miseries; but that also failed. Lastly, she decided to let the little baby live. Now he was growing up, and soon was to become a big man, get his education in big institutions, then become a Member of Parliament, a lawyer, a doctor, an engineer......

The baby finished suckling and Nkatha buttoned her blouse. "My boy, sleep now," she said.

"Will he sleep with all this noise and commotion?" her Aunt asked, after overhearing Nkatha talk to the child. Mogambi bent his head forward and, as he strained to look in her direction, he exhibited embarrassment and regret.

The ceremony came to an end. The graduands, tutors and guests stood up for the last prayer. After the prayer Nkatha, her Aunt and Mogambi started walking out of the college field. Along the way Nkatha took a photo with her wreath and certificate. She also took one with her baby and Aunt. Mogambi hanged around, chagrined. When they were at the gate Mogambi started up a conversation.

"It is great for you to graduate, Nkatha."

"No doubt about that," she retorted

"You are going to be a teacher and you will earn a salary every month."

"The money will be for me and my baby," she said and clasped her baby closely to her bosom, kissing him on the lips, neck and face.

Nkatha knew she was being rude to him. He deserves it, she thought. He rejected me when I needed him most... I have suffered immense stress due to that rejection. Had it not been for the college principal who understood my plight and allowed me to take courses as a day scholar, my education could have been jeopardized and I could not have come this far. Had he accepted me, I could have moved in to stay with him. Instead of comfort and happiness, he brought misery to my life…. I hate him! I hate him! devil… devil …devil…devil….

"Nkatha, why are you so sad," her Aunt interrupted her thoughts.

"I am not sad, Aunt," she spoke, somehow squirmed, then held her baby high up on her head.

"Baby, baby, sweet baby…"

"But I thought you had said you wanted to meet Mogambi today?" she spoke in a low voice, close to Nkatha's ears.

"No. I don't want to talk to him."

"But, have you not been longing for this day? Have you not been waiting to meet with him?" She ignored her.

"You truly look sad," Mogambi added.

"How can I be sad when I am with my son?" she told Mogambi, then curled her lower lip in contempt.

"Do you think you can get time to talk to me some time next week?"

"Time? Eh! No time. I am busy," she spoke firmly, bitterness and defiance in her voice.

"Then kindly give me your number?" he almost pleaded. "Maybe I can call to find out when you are free."

"No. I am not free. I will never be free."

"Ok? Maybe I can make a surprise visit to your place one of these days."

"No. Don't dare come to my house. You are not allowed."

"As a friend, of course."

"No. You are not a friend."

"To see my baby," Mogambi insisted.

"Which baby?" Nkatha's voice rose.

"This one."

"This one?" she asked with fury, veins forming on her temples. "But I thought you had said it belonged to somebody else, didn't you, Mogambi?"

"Calm down, Nkatha," her Aunt spoke as she moved closer to her, holding her shoulder.

"You said you were not the father. You rejected the boy even before he was born!" she shouted at him, attracting everyone who was passing by. People stopped to look. "You rejected him." The baby whimpered and touched his mother's head. Nkatha looked down at him. "Baby, peace! Peace, baby!" she smiled at the baby. "All I have is you, baby. Baby, peace. Peace, baby."

Her Aunt pulled Nkatha's hand away and whispered: "Nkatha, you had planned to meet with Mogambi today, didn't you?"

"No, Aunt"

"But you had said you wanted to mend things with him, didn't you?"

Nkatha ignored her, releasing her hand from her grip. When they reached the bus stage, her Aunt bid Mogambi bye. "Bye, Aunt," Mogambi responded. Nkatha also said bye to him and spat contemptuously beside him. She clasped her baby close to her chest and left. As she walked, she turned the baby's head away from Mogambi's direction. "Baby, don't look at someone who rejected you." Mogambi looked on and felt humiliated.

Nkatha left Mogambi standing there, spellbound, stunned and crushed. He deserves it, she thought. She walked on defiantly, carrying in her head her future, the future of her child, a future crammed with achievements and fulfillment. With sufficient finance and a teaching career, she seemed to ride on top of the world, waves of joy and delight all weaving in and around her. But somewhere under her subconscious, she felt some emptiness, a vacuum, a space that was hollow and frightening.

On the periphery of that hollow space stood Mogambi, tall and handsome, staring into her new-found world of happiness. She felt the absence of him, of his role as the father of her son. She once loved him and even now, as she walked on she knew she still loved him. She had come to meet him today, to mend the broken fences with him, but without reason she had changed her mind.

Now, as she walked along, without him, she felt lost, scattered in the dark emptiness of space, carrying with her a life of no purpose and aim. She suddenly stopped, threw down her boy, turned round and started running back. She ran across the vast field on which they had walked, shouting "Mogambi! Mogambi! Mogambi! Stop! Wait!" She reached the main road where they had bid Mogambi goodbye. To her chagrin she saw his figure disappearing into a bus he had boarded and the bus sped off. She desperately sprung towards it, screaming "Mogambi! Mogambi! Stop, Mogambi!" She flew fast beside the road, her eyes fixed on the vehicle that carried her man.

She was about to give up when the vehicle slowed down and came to a halt beside the road. Nkatha increased her speed towards it, panting and sweating as she made one last effort to reach it. Mogambi alighted and the bus zoomed off. He walked back towards Nkatha. Both reached each other and she fell headlong on his chest.

"Mogambi," she stammered, panting, holding onto him tightly around the waist. Her Aunt, who was following behind with the baby, reached them.

"Stop crying, Nkatha," he said as he tenderly smoothed her hair.

"Mogambi. I love you. I have always loved you. I still love you. You are the one who walked out on me."

"Sorry about what happened, Nkatha," he apologized, his words sounding like balm on her heart. "Forgive me. I am very sorry"

"Mogambi, how do I forgive you?"

"Forgive me, Nkatha. I am yours. You are mine. We were both meant for each other," he was nearly sobbing himself.

Aunt looked on with amazement as the two lovers kissed, caressed, patted, sobbed and screamed, washing each other with their own tears and saliva. Nkatha suddenly stopped, disentangled herself from Mogambi and turned to Aunt, took her child from her and handed him to Mogambi. She then turned to Aunt: "You can go now, Aunt," she shook her hand as a gesture of gratitude. "Thank you for everything, Aunt. I will always remember you for everything."

It was dusk and the sun had long sunken into the horizon, leaving behind romantic orange paint on the blue-washed sky. The two lovers gently walked through the scattered woods on the tall tender grass towards the west side of the city where Mogambi owned a mansion.

The Weeds

"The weeds! The weeds!" Langa't raved and shook his head. "We must uproot them!"

"Uproot them?" Cherono asked, disbelief wrinkling her forehead. "Which weeds?"

"The weeds ! The invaders! The stinking tribe!"

"You mean the Kikuyu people?"

"Yes, the Kikuyu! We must wipe them out this time round, "Lang'at roared and shook his head in fierce display of anger. He dashed into the house and picked his machete and came out foaming with a murderous fury. He wielded the machete and slashed the air with it. "The weeds!!" he slashed again, cut, pierced and prodded the air with it. "The weeds! We must cut them off our land."

"What do you plan to do with them?" Cherono asked with concern, placed the bamboo tray on the ground and rose up to her feet.

"We already know what to do with them"

"You can't kill them, can you?

"We know. Women shouldn't know. Women only need to sit in the kitchen and wait to hear what happens," he said, dismissing his wife.

"They have a right to be here," Cherono said authoritatively. "They came here many years ago and this, now, is their land. Most of them were born here. Their children were born here. Where else do you want them to go? They have a right to be here, Lang'at," she said and bent down to blow off chaff from the millet in the tray.

"They have a right? Which right?"

"Yes, they have a right. Their land was taken away by the colonial *muzungu*, and they were given this one. It is not their fault."

"The *Muzungu* left, they also should leave our land."

"But they have no home to go back to."

"Their people should give them the land the *Muzungu* left behind."

"The land was taken away. It is many decades ago."

"That is none of our business."

Suddenly Lang'at jumped up as if a sharp object pricked his feet. With a sudden startling yell, he sprang onto his feet and flew off towards the banana plantation.

"Papa, wait!" Kiambaa, his 10-year old son, called, and ran after him. His papa stopped and looked back. "Papa, please go with me!"

"No-o-o!" he bawled from a distant. Kiambaa stopped, and tears coursed down his cheeks. "You must remain at home. Do not go anywhere as these are volatile times! Bloody times! Dangerous times my son!"

Kiambaa turned back, his hand kneading his eyeballs. He was the only child of his father. Due to medical problems his mother could not give birth to another child after he was born. Being the only child of his parents, Kiambaa was loved and pampered. He was showered with presents and gifts.

Kiambaa turned his head to steal a glimpse of his father. His father's bulging body, tattered coat and old hat were swallowed by dark green foliage of the banana plantation. He disappeared into the woods, the machete swirling viciously in his hand. He was later spotted climbing up the hill on the other side of the river, then shortly disappeared among the rocks.

"Ma--," Kiambaa called when he returned to the house. "You mean father is going to fight the Kikuyu people?"

"Who told you about the fight, Kiambaa?" his mother asked, surprise in her voice.

"The imminent fight is everywhere. People talk about it all over. Before schools closed pupils spoke about the war against the Kikuyu."

"Yes, you are right, Kiambaa. They want the Kikuyu to go back to their homes and vacate our land."

"Do you also believe it is the correct thing to do, Ma?"

"Not really, they are part of us. They were born here. It is not proper to expel them, or even to hate them."

"I feel the same, Ma," Kiambaa spoke with concern.

"Your father cannot be stopped. He and the others are set."

"My friend, Kamau is a Kikuyu," Kiambaa said, and shut his mouth in a gesture of fear and uncertainty. "Ma, let me go and see Kamau at their home." Before his Mother could warn him of the danger he could face, Kiambaa had already flown along the path that led into the maize plantation.

"Kiambaa! Come back here!" his Mother called. "It is not safe to be out there alone!" His black trousers disappeared into the maize plantation. He ran through the path and reached a bigger path that ran down to the river. He followed it. He crossed a single-plank bridge and, without fear, Kiambaa climbed up the steep hill that led to Kamau's home. He reached the homestead and stood at the fence. It was all quiet.

Suddenly he heard a voice from the banana plantation: "Little boy, whom do you want? The family is not here. They have gone to hide in the church on top of the hill." He held his breath and explored the maize plantation around. He came face to face with an old woman, seated, meditatively smoking her pipe.

"Grandma, what are you doing there alone?"

"They have gone and left me behind," she said. "I could be killed if found in the house."

"What did you say?"

"Our people, the Kikuyu, are hiding in the church up the hill."

"Why, grandma?"

"Your people will kill them if they found them."

"In the church?"

"Yes, there they can't be touched by warriors from your community."

"And why do they want to kill them?"

"Oh, my grandson, you won't understand," she said and inserted the pipe into her lips and continued smoking meditatively.

"And where is my friend Kamau?"

"He and his mother were the last ones to leave."

Kiambaa stood still, looking at the home of Kamau. He was a great friend. Both were in standard four and the teachers referred to them as twins. They sat together on one desk in class. They also got almost the same marks in most of their exams. They arrived in school at the same time and left together in the evening. They visited each other's home during the weekends and their parents cooked food for them and loved them. Now their friendship was uncertain. They could not understand why there were differences between their people. Kiambaa looked at the once-playing ground outside Kamau's home and his eyes moistened.

"My grandchild," the old woman called from her abode in the maize plantation. "Go home and avoid trouble."

"I will go and look for Kamau," Kiambaa retorted, his voice shed with defiance.

"Don't go up the hill, you hear?"

"I will go and look for my friend," he said and flew up the dark woods on the steep hillside. He ran all the way through the dark forest up the path that led to the fence where the gate of the church lay open. He stopped and peered into the church precinct. It was empty and quiet. No one was in sight. He stood and stared about. He then heard a thin whiff of song being blown over the fence by the wind. It was emanating from the church. People were singing "Alleluia!" He stealthily walked through the corrugated iron gate and stood in the open field. He swept his eyes over the compound of the church but did not understand why there was no one around. The song from the church increased in volume and he could get every word they were singing. He gathered courage and walked towards the open door of the huge building that stood in the vast field like a monster. He stopped at the door and peeped inside. About forty people, mostly women and children, sat hurdled together, mumbling a song—or were they moaning. Kamau, who sat among the crowd, caught Kiambaa's figure. Kiambaa waved at him and at once Kamau sprung to his feet and elbowed his way through the crowd. He ran towards the door. They grabbed each other and embraced. After a short while, Kamau took him in to join the singing congregation.

Once inside, Kiambaa realized that the people were nervous and worried. Children cried of hunger, while old people dosed on the cold floor. "God will help us," one of them said.

"They will fear coming into the church as this is a holy ground!" another one added.

"No one has ever done evil to the church!" more voices joined in.

Kiambaa swept his eyes over the haggard faces; he felt pity for them. "Why should people suffer so?" he asked himself. He squeezed his small body among the women and sung happily with them. He touched the crying babies and wiped their tears as a way of comforting them. When the babies cried he felt like crying with them.

Meanwhile, Lang'at and his accomplices hurried up the hill. "Hurry up, you lazy bones!" he commanded. Carrying gallons of petrol, spears, arrows and machetes, they camouflaged themselves with leaves and tendrils as they walked through the woods. They finally reached the church. The men at once fell upon it with hammers and nails. In a split second the church doors and windows were reinforced with rafters. The song "Alleluia" intensified in the church. Ululation and cheers for Jesus rose, punctuated with screams of terror and fear.

"Help!" voices burst out.

"Jesus come down now!" they called in song.

"Jesus, you are our protector!" they shouted their hopes.

"Pour the petrol! Pour!" Lang'at shouted his orders in urgency. Petrol was sprinkled over the walls, windows, doors and the roof. "Now move back!" he shouted his command. He lit the match stick and threw it over the roof of the huge building. It caught fire. The men scampered backwards and disappeared into the maize plantation.

Lang'at ran, panting through the dark woods, down the hill, into the valley. He was perspiring and breathing heavily. He looked back and saw a ball of fire rolling over the once-magnificent building. When he reached home, he threw his weight down on the three-legged stool and said: "The weeds! The weeds are up in flames!"

"Lang'at," Cherono called from the kitchen. "Have you done anything wrong, my husband?"

"Wrong? Why wrong?" he asked.

"Your eyes are red my husband," she said with concern.

"Anything I do I do for the sake of our children, and grand children, so that they have better life afterwards."

"Lang'at, you look worn out."

"Yes, I have uprooted the weeds! I have burnt the weeds! I have thrown away the weeds!" He exulted, his face foaming with rage. He moved out of the house and stood outside. Cherono joined him. He cast his eyes towards the hill. "Look yonder! The fire! The weeds burning! The stinking weeds! The justice we have craved for long! The truth that we have sought for years!"

Cherono peered into the distant and was amazed. Her mouth gaping, she lowered her head and gazed at Lang'at's face as though a little leopard perched there. "Wow! Lang'at, what have you done to the church?"

"Nothing more than just ridding it of the weeds,'" he said calmly. "I have done it for, for, for—by the way where is Kiambaa, my lovely son?" he asked. The question seemed to startle him. He turned black as if the devil haunted him. He stood, transfixed on the spot, staring blankly like someone in a dream, misgivings and foreboding weaving around him.

"Gone to see his friend, Kamau," she answered.

"Gone to see his friend, Kamau? The weeds' son? Where can he be now? My beloved son," he asked, peered into the empty space and sought for an answer. His head hung heavy upon him. He shook it and suddenly sprung to his feet, and flew out towards the banana plantation. He ran down the field and reached the river.

He crossed it and panted up the hill. He finally reached Kamau's home. He stood at the fence and peered into the homestead. The home was quiet like a grave yard. Birds sung from among the boughs that shed an ominous shadow outside the ground. Lang'at listened to the birds and wondered why their chirps made him want to sob. As he stood still he heard, from among the plantation, a thin voice of a woman saying: "There is no body there, Chief Lang'at. They have all gone to church up the hill." He was taken aback with the strange voice. He looked towards the plantation. An old woman sat in the banana plantation, smoking her pipe. Lang'at looked at her and sympathized. He could not kill her. She looked too old to be killed.

"And Kiambaa, my beloved son, have you seen him?"

"The little boy?"

"Yes, the little boy."

"He was here sometimes ago. He walked up the hill, probably to the church."

"What?" he asked, his eyes bulging out.

"He walked up to the church"

"To the church? " he shouted and was on his feet, crashing the grass, plants, trees and anything before him, on his way up the hill. "Kiambaa! Oh, my beloved son! My only child!" He cried as he climbed up the hill. "Kiambaa! Oh, my only child!"

When he reached the church, smoke was already engulfing the building. A few faces watched from a safe distance behind the fences. "Kiambaa-a-a-a-a-a! Kiambaa-a-a-a-a-a-!" he called, panick-stricken. He ran round the building like a dog with rabies. He shook like a leaf in the wind. He foamed from the corner of his mouth like a sick chicken. Few people came to his help. They ran to the nearby villages and brought buckets with them. They fetched water from the nearby tap and well and sprinkled it on the building, but the brick wall, grille doors and windows could hear none of it. Some climbed up the roof and poured water on it, but the corrugated iron sheets defied their effort. They embarked on cutting the rafters that reinforced the doors and windows, but, they too, blazed with fierce fire.

Confusion and commotion could be heard from the building. Movements of people, desperate voices calling for help, blended with songs and prayers, spilled out of the building.

The old man threw himself down and started eating blades of grass like a goat. "My son, my only child!" he screamed. He sprung up, stripped himself naked and ran round the building like a lunatic. People shut their eyes in embarrassment. He climbed up the wall of the building and reached the roof. He started pulling iron sheets with his bare hands. He managed to weaken one sheet which he

tore like a piece of cloth. He looked into the dark inferno of flames. "Kiambaa-a-a-a!" he bawled. His bushy beard caught fire and it was singed. "Kiambaa-a-a-a-a-a!" he called.

"Papa-a-a-!" a thin voice finally rose amid the flames. "Kiamba-a-a-a!"

"Papa, I am burning!"

Lang'at peered into the blaze. He could see the weeds running here and there, carrying with them balls of fire. Others sat, helpless, waiting for death to consume them. Children clang to their mothers while the old women and men helplessly raised their hands to God.

"Kiambaa-a-a-a!" he called again. "Are you alive, my son? My only child!" Tears welled down his cheeks.

"Papa, I am burning! Papa!" a voice rose again amid

the clamour. It then died gradually. He peered keenly into the sea of fire. Was it Kiambaa he saw snuggled into the corner of the house, clinging onto women's skirts and screaming for their help? Is it Kiambaa he saw raising his hands up to his papa? Is it Kiambaa he saw turning amorphous into a wild ball of fire?

"Kiambaa-a-a-a!" he called desperately, tears washing his cheeks.

"Papa!" the voice had become thinner and indistinct.

"Kiambaa, my beloved son! My only child!" he shouted.

"The weeds, papa!" a voice came, and died away.

"The weeds, Kiambaa!" he mumbled to himself.

"The weeds, Papa!" a distant echo rose among the flames.

The weeds, my beloved son!"

The old man could no longer see his son as the sparks and smoke filled the dark space below. He called upon the people to get him a rope. Someone ran in for a rope and threw it up to the roof for him. He unwound it and let the tip of it descend down into the dark pit. As Lang'at tried to lower it to reach his beloved son, his hands lost their grip on the timber support he clutched and he fell headlong into the hollow sea of fire. People quickly closed their eyes in panic. They clutched their cheeks in terror. They stood transfixed as if thunderbolt had struck them.

Years later, when the church was re-constructed, the people carved letters on a stone, which they placed at the entrance, that read:

This is a Church
Where Chief Lang'at
And His 10-Year Old Kiambaa
Burnt to Death
Among the Weeds.

Nduku

Nduku saw a tears-gas canister flying in the air; it then hit the ground beside her, exuding smoke, she cowered. Panic-stricken, she jumped up from a stone on which she was seated and started running, leaving behind her wares. She heard several gun-shots behind her, accentuated by wails and screams. Looking back, she saw people running in her direction. She increased speed along Spine Road. The road was empty. No vehicle was in sight. The traders who sold second –hand items beside the road were not there. Shops had been closed and the Spine Road petrol station, the only petrol station along that road, was not operational.

"I wish I knew this was going to happen," she said to herself, bit her lower lip in regret as she kept running along. Her husband had advised her not to go out to sell her wares that morning. There was still tension since the presidential election results had been announced three days earlier. "What will my children eat?" she defied his advice. "Let me go. I can't watch as my children die of hunger." Her husband shrugged his shoulders and gave her free reign.

On the day election results were announced ten people had been killed in the market where she had now been selling her second-hand clothes. This happened when supporters of Orange Democratic Movement party clashed with supporters of Party of National Unity. Shops and kiosks were broken into and properties looted. Women were raped and children were hurt in the ensuing commotion. The following day it was reported that a bus carrying eighty people from Western province had been stopped at a barricade along Nakuru-Nairobi road and passengers beaten, frisked and women raped. The situation was volatile and Nduku's husband had misgivings as she left the home that morning.

She veered from Spine Road, and started walking slowly along a by-way that ran between Victory Church and Precious Gift School. She suddenly stopped. Ahead of her she saw a big crowd of men singing a political chant, waving sticks and swords. She stood still. A violent trembling seized and shook her. She quickly ducked towards an abandoned building by the road side. She climbed the circular stairs to the first floor and stood behind a wall, looking down to the road below. Her heart beat in her like a hammer. She looked around the dusty room. There were scattered crumbs of old crusted faeces on the floor; dead bats still hung from the empty ceiling. The air was filled with urine. She took her eyes from the room and looked down the path.

The men were now right below the building, their songs and chants rose up clear to Nduku's ears. They wielded their swords, cried for the blood of their opponents and beat the air with their swords and machetes.

Nduku watched, her heart beating like a roll of drums, clutching the stone-wall with both of her hands. The wall on which her body clung felt cold. She detached her stomach from it. The men, some of whom were half-naked, wore feather-hats, and had their stomachs, arms and legs tattooed. They cried "PNU! PNU! PNU!" as they marched along. Nduku watched and her heart beat faster. She feared they might see her and they would come into the building to get her. She would then be flogged and, in the end, raped and abandoned for dead.

She opened her eyes, and looked below. Before the men were out of the vicinity, another group of men had emerged from the other side of the road, singing and chanting "ODM! ODM! ODM!" They too were wielding swords and sticks and charging forward, provoking this other group. They called them all sorts of names: Cowards! Nincompoops! Broomsticks! Imbeciles!

The men in this other group were enraged. They gathered stones from Murram Road and positioned themselves ready to strike. They breathed fire and brimstone, swore and took oath. Then at once they descended upon the other group with stones, chasing them along the road towards Spine Road. Nduku looked and saw three men tripping to the ground, as hails of stones, sticks and clubs fell upon them. In a split second the men were dead. Nduku clutched her temples and shuddered. Shortly, a police Landrover pulled up beside the dead bodies. The men, from both parties, dispersed. The policemen looked on as the last person disappeared into the dark alleys. They bundled the dead bodies into the vehicle. Before it zoomed off, one policeman pointed towards the building in which Nduku hid. "Some could be hiding in this building!" he said. Nduku panicked and froze by the wall. Her heart filled with horror, she quickly threw herself flat on the floor, and then cautiously crawled on her stomach up to the foot of the staircase. She then crawled up and reached the next floor of the building. She rose behind a wall and peeped through an empty window down to the road. None of the policemen had come up to search. Shortly the engine of the vehicle started, and Nduku saw it zoom off.

Nduku peered at the road, her mind blank. There was no danger. She climbed down the stairs with caution, looking in all directions for imminent danger. It was now getting dark. She had to go home with nothing for the children; she had not sold anything from her wares when the commotion broke out. Furthermore, her wares would not be recovered; street urchins will thank God

for that day.

She had to find a short cut to her home in Komarock Phase Two, and avoid using the main road and the main streets that might lead her into trouble. She followed a small path between PCEA Church and Komarock Primary School and ran along it. When she had gone almost a hundred meters, she bumped into a woman who was walking in the opposite direction but was dressed in black. The woman exhibited panic upon seeing Nduku. None of them talked, but went past each other and then, at a safe distant, each turned to look behind.

Nduku was suddenly filled with fear as she hurried alone in the darkness along the path. Previously a woman was reported to have been raped by a gang of the outlawed Singi Singi sect on the same foot-path. Had she forgotten the incident that was reported on TV in broad daylight? Nduku's heart closed in panic. She could have followed the main road or the main street as they didn't habour serious danger, except for the police patrol. It was now very dark, and it had started drizzling. It would be half an hour before Nduku reached home. She started sweating out of fear. She didn't know why her heart sank, and why she was filled with horror. She didn't understand why she felt like screaming for help. She walked fast, listening and looking in all directions.

Suddenly, as her sixth sense had been warning her all along, Nduku bumped into a figure in the darkness. "Ouch!" she exclaimed and jumped back. Her throat closed in panic.

"Don't scream!" the man warned. His voice sent the blood firing through Nduku's cold body. "If you scream—" he spoke and wielded his sword. Sweat broke out on her smooth brow and the palms of her hands grew clammy with cold terror. Nduku froze. The man seized her arm, and dragged her along towards a small cramped dark house beside the path. Her hands were tingling with terror and horror. His grip was strong. Nduku could not manage to wring herself from it. "If you scream—" he warned again and placed the glimmering sword on her neck, and Nduku tasted the bitter dung of fear.

The confined dark room smelled of cigarette smoke, beer and opium. Dimly lit by a kerosene lamp, Nduku could make out other figures in the dark room, seated somewhere in the corner. They were five men, all wearing hats that covered their foreheads and part of their eyes, sipping something like whisky. Tears streamed down Nduku's eyes. She trembled like a goat caught for slaughter. The man's grip on her arm loosened. "Sit down here," he commanded. "If you scream, see—" he brought a glinting sword before her face again. When Nduku hesitated to sit, the man pushed her down onto a chair. One of the men seated at the corner came to his feet; he came and stood before Nduku. Nduku trembled and her heart was filled with horror and terror. He placed his hand on her shoulder, and then pinched her breast. He then bent down and bit her ear with his teeth. Nduku froze. She wanted to scream-- but how far out will her voice go?

Will her husband and the policemen be looking for her? Definitely, yes, but will they trace and find her? It was difficult to trace her whereabouts. She was doomed, she thought. Nduku resigned to her fate.

The man who kidnapped her went out of the room. The other man who had pinched her breast also followed him out. The other three men were lounging at the corner and seemed too drunk to even stand on their feet. Nduku watched them. In the glimmering light they looked gaunt and eerie, like vampires. Something crossed her mind. She had to escape. She had to be brave enough. She gathered courage.

She was still planning her escape when suddenly the two men returned, accompanied by two other men. They carried with them polythene papers: eggs, loaves of bread, kerosene for their stove and vegetables for their supper. Would they ask her to prepare supper for them? Nduku wondered what was going to happen to her. Her fate hung in the balance. Her mind went blank. How was she going to run away from such strong men? Won't she risk her life?

One of the men snuffed out the kerosene lamp. They all sat in utter darkness. What were they up to? Why had they put off the lamp? Nduku wondered. Whispers and murmurings filled the dark room. Hustles and rustles followed. Then silence descended upon the room. Then suddenly sinister movements around the room began again. Nduku's heart beat harder. The hour had come and she had to face it with courage. Could she find the door? Could she put up a fight? What, with all those knives, swords? She stood up and again sat in panic. She fidgeted in her chair. She wanted to spring up on her feet and fly out, reach the road and rent the dark night with a scream. Maybe people would run in and her captors will be confused and let her go.

One man walked to the door and bolted it. Another was moving towards Nduku. Nduku stood up and gathered courage. She moved away from her chair. "Don't try any games, you hear?" a voice in the dark room boomed in her ears. Then a clammy hand grabbed her frail arm and dragged her to the corner of the dark room. Nduku screamed, but a heavy hand came to her mouth, muffling the voice.

Another hand held her by the torso and threw her on what Nduku felt was an old dirty musty mattress on which was spread a mouldy blanket. Before Nduku could think of her last remedy that was to save her life, the man tore her blouse, skirt and pants—all at one go. Immediately she became a whirlwind of arms and legs and sharp raking teeth and fingernails. The man lost his hold and clutched a badly bitten finger, cursing. Nduku attempted to come to her feet, but the man threw himself on her and slapped her cheeks. He then punched her face several times and Nduku collapsed.

The morning came. Nduku was startled from her slumber. She didn't know where she was. Beside her were two policemen, her husband and her two daughters, Mbithe and Mukuru. "Are you okay?" her husband asked. Nduku was too exhausted to talk. She could not lift herself from the small mattress on which she lay. She didn't understand where she was and what she was doing there. Why had the policemen come to fetch her? She lay there and was unable to turn herself.

Shortly Nduku strained her eyes open. She was able to see her husband, Mbithe and Mukuru. "Mama," the seven-year old Mbithe cried. Nduku recognized her daughter's voice and moved her head. Mbithe sat beside her and caressed her mother's dirty unkempt tuft of hair.

Nduku's husband moved closer, tongue-tied and silent. "Are you able to see us now?" one police officer asked her.

Nduku was carried from the small mattress in that stuffy room and bundled into the police vehicle and rushed to the Kenyatta National Hospital. She was admitted to Intensive Care Unit. By evening she was able to recognize the people around her, but was not able to recall what had happened. All she remembered was that she had gone to the market on that day and got kidnapped. What happened after that was hard to recall. The following day came and Nduku was still receiving medication. Finally she recalled how it all happened and how she was raped by a gang of men.

On the third day, Nduku heard that the gang had been arrested by the policemen. She was carried from her hospital bed to go to the Central Police Station to identify them from a parade. At the station, she was asked to come forward and pick those she saw that night. Nduku did not hesitate and neither did she have difficulties identifying them. She looked over the faces that stood bold before her. She picked all of them five at one go. One thin man with a thin chin had a moustache. Another one was stout, with a round face with cropped hair. The third was medium size, with small narrow eyes.

The Street Dogs

A mixture of honks, sirens, and yells from *matatu* conductors was deafening. There was pushing and shoving, people hurrying past while others hanging about; many others were boarding and others alighting from buses and *matatus*. Bicycles, motorbikes and *mkokoteni* hand carts burrowed through the mass of people. The sun overhead was scorching and Moraa's face burned. A flurry of dust flew about, anyhow, engulfing them; they quickly could close their eyes, then wiped their faces from time to time. Moraa squeezed through a wall of human bodies, holding tightly onto her Mother's hand, while feeling Aunt Kemunto's basket. They came onto an open space in the middle of tall storeyed buildings and felt relieved from the overcrowded street they had left behind. Suddenly Moraa cringed in terror, tightly clinging onto her Mother's skirt. "Street dogs, Mummy! Dogs!" she cried, pointing towards two lunatic, burly, unkempt men nearby. One of them was chewing meat from a dirty bone and the other was scavenging in the dustbin that was overflowing with litter and flies. "Street dogs!" she clasped tightly onto her Mother's dress. Aunt Kemunto held Moraa back, placed her hand round her nape and smiled.

"Those are not dogs," Aunt Kemunto corrected her. "One of them is your uncle, the other a teacher."

"The one dipping his hand into the litter bin is Rayori, a brother to your father," her mother explained. "And the other one leaning against the post was formerly a teacher in one of the local schools at our home. His name is Omweri."

"So, why are they here, Mummy?" Moraa asked, a puzzle wrinkling up his forehead.

"The story is long, Moraa," her mother said.

"Tell me, just tell me Mummy," she insisted as she loosened her grip on her Mother's dress, while peering anxiously at the two men.

"You want to know, Moraa?" Aunt Kemunto asked, smiling. She bent her tall figure down to reach her, and whispered: "It is a long story dear…In our village there lived people from the Abanyire, a tribe from the neighbouring country. They came over half a century ago and bought pieces of land amidst us. They lived with us for all that time. Then in the year two thousand and seven, when you were a baby, able to crawl, something happened between them and our people."

"Something? What?"

"Yes, something," Aunt Kemunto continued and looked towards Moraa's Mother for approval. Moraa's Mother turned her head and looked to the direction of the two burly men. One of the men threw himself on the ground and sprawled his huge body across the dust, slithering like a snake, while throwing up his enormous soot-coated bone to the air and letting it fall directly into his fly-invested mouth. The other man stood, smiling at himself, picking lice from his sisal-thick hair and throwing the invisible insects into his mouth. Moraa stood, her mouth agape, amazed.

"Now, tell me," she turned to her Aunt."What happened, Aunt?"

Aunt Kemunto: Our men assembled one night, without fear.

Mother Moraa: Each came with a bow, an arrow and a spear.

Aunt Kemunto: These people took our land, one man said.

Mother Moraa: It is time they left, the second man said.

Aunt Kemunto: They razed down their huts and granaries.

Mother Moraa: They uprooted their maize and their berries.

Aunt Kemunto: They raped their women.

Mother Moraa: They maimed their men.

Aunt Kemunto: Then they killed the people.

Mother Moraa: Causing a political ripple

Aunt Kemunto: The people sprawled on fields, dead.

Mother Moraa: They lay on farms like people in bed.

Aunt Kemunto: Blood so cold and red.

Mother Moraa: Upon paths was shed.

Aunt Kemunto: They looted their furniture, food and cooking pots.

Mother Moraa: And took away from them sheep, cows and goats.

Aunt Kemunto: As they left, they ransacked their smouldering huts.

Mother Moraa: And out of the huts fled lizards, mice and rats.

Aunt Kemunto: Causing turbulence, commotion and a big ripple.

Mother Moraa: It caused tension among the people.

Aunt Kemunto: Our men came home with Abanyire people's heads.

Mother Moraa: Kept them as trophies of victory under their beds.

Aunt Kemunto: They sang songs of victory.

Mother Moraa: They had set a village history.

Aunt Kemunto: Little did they know the repercussions.

Mother Moraa: That one day they would learn the lessons.

Aunt Kemunto: The street dogs.

Mother Moraa: The growling dogs.

"Stop, mother! Stop!" Moraa shouted at her Mother, and pulled her Aunt's dress, anger flashing through her small eyes. "How can all that happen, Mummy?"

"But it happened, Moraa," her mother roared with remorseful anger, beads of tears dancing on her eyeballs as she reminisced the historical event she had narrated with her sister.

"The story is unbelievable, Mother," Moraa cried.

"You are right——," Aunt Kemunto nodded her head.

"It can only be possible in a movie, Mother." Moraa's face was filled with the horror and the terror of the events in the story as just narrated by her Mother and Aunt Kemunto.

"You are right, Moraa," Aunt Kemunto responded. "The event of that historical period sound like fiction."

"That is why your uncle Rayori and that teacher are both here," her mother explained. "They did what was abominable, unacceptable."

"They--what do you mean?" Moraa started, got confused and stopped.

"You see—you are still young. You need to grow in order to understand how it happens when you do evil to your fellow man," her Mother said.

"The huts of the Abanyire which they razed down," Aunt Kemunto began, "they planted vegetables on the ashes and remains of their burnt wood; when it grew they consumed it."

"Is it wrong?"

"Yes, it is wrong. If you do evil by burning someone's house, you better be careful not to eat anything that grows on the remains of the burnt wood, nor should you drink water from the streams that flow through the ashes of the burnt hut or nearby; otherwise you will become lunatic from *amaera*, the evil of arson."

"That is what our people did; they burnt the huts of Abanyire and later ate vegetables and drunk water from the ground where they burnt the houses," Mother Moraa clarified.

"Oh--"

"Our people also killed and maimed the Abanyire people without reason," Mother Moraa continued. "They had done nothing untoward to us. They were innocent. They had lived with us for half a century, and had become like our sisters and brothers. Some even spoke our tongue, while others married our daughters and some of our daughters eloped with their randy men, so that we had become one people and one blood."

"When you kill an innocent person, who has not done you any wrong, there are repercussions," Aunt Kemunto said remorsefully. "You suffer from *oborominta*, or *chimuma*."

"So, what—," Moraa stammered, puzzled.

"And this *chimuma*," Aunt Kemunto continued, "will need you to undergo *ogokoreranwa*, a cleansing ritual that thwarts evil, then you could be forgiven and could be allowed to share food and other items with others in the community."

"So your uncle and the teacher you see here," her mother picked from where Aunt Kemunto had left, "killed innocent people, and they never went through *ogokoreranwa*, the cleansing ritual, which requires the slaughtering of bulls and the sharing of the meat and blood with the bereaved members of those they killed. Instead of undergoing the cleansing ritual, your uncle and the teacher you see there, and many others as well, started sharing foods and other items with the bereaved members of those they killed. They drunk water that streamed from and ran through the ground on which Abanyire houses stood before they were razed down; they also ate vegetables planted and grown upon the soil on which the razed houses collapsed; worse still, they built their own houses using posts, iron sheets and thatch grass recovered from the houses of Abanyire people that they razed down. Now they are suffering from *chimuma*. Chimuma turns you, your children and your grandchildren mad."

"Now Mummy—," Moraa started speaking, but was unable to utter a word, and when she found the words she said: "When I grow up, Mummy, I can't kill; neither will I maim anybody in my life. I won't burn someone's house, be it of my tribe or of someone from another tribe," she spoke, and her face darkened with remorse. "I will live in peace with the Abaryire people, and all other tribes living in our land."

"Living in peace with everyone else has its benefits," Aunt Kemunto said.

"It benefits development," Mother Moraa added.

"I would like to form a peace club among the youth in our community," Moraa thought aloud. "to promote and advance peace in our area. I want as many youth as possible to join me."

"A peace club? That is a good idea," Aunt Kemunto nodded her head.

"I will call it Youth for Peace Initiative."

"Great idea, Moraa," her Mother spoke enthusiastically.

Gr-r-r-r-r-r-r-iiiil" the street dogs growled, and passers-by scampered. Startled, Moraa grabbed her Mother's skirt again. "Gr-r-r-r-r-r-r-rriiiil! " the dogs charged against the surging crowd. One man picked a stone and hurled it at the dogs. Another one picked a stick and aimed it at one of the dogs and hit it on the head. Moraa, her mother and Aunt Kemunto quickly moved away from the scene and walked through a narrow alley that snaked between two tall buildings and went away.